The Nature and the Name of Love

The Nature and the Name of Love

Religion for the Contemporary World

Martin Forward

EPWORTH

Copyright © Martin Forward 2008

The Author has asserted his right under the Copyright,
Designs and Patents Act, 1988, to be
identified as the Author of this Work

British Library Cataloguing in Publication data

A catalogue record for this book is available
from the British Library

978 0 7162 0637 8

First published in 2008
by Epworth
4 John Wesley Road
Werrington
Peterborough PE4 6ZP

Typeset by Regent Typesetting, London
Printed and bound in Great Britain by
MPG Books Ltd, Bodmin, Cornwall

Contents

Introduction and Acknowledgements

A number of colleagues and students have asked me what this book is about. To some I have responded that it attempts to rescue the notion that God has a place in religious studies. They have usually looked at me rather oddly, muttered a polite comment and moved away swiftly, leaving behind their distinct though non-verbal impression that dottiness was leading me to elaborate the obvious. To others, I have expressed the (somewhat impertinent) desire to liberate God, both from some of his most ardent yet unpleasant supporters and also from some of his noisiest yet often clueless and trivial critics. Occasionally I have, with only slight exaggeration, told enquirers that interpreting religion as the study of clearly defined faith-institutions, which one can choose to join or not as one sees fit, is a strange modern European and North American invention, and that I would like to show why this innovation makes most westerners unable to understand the dynamic and sometimes scary faith of people from other cultures.

The book is all these things, and a few more. Chapter 1 asks whether religion has a future in Western Europe and other lands where secular and sceptical European thought has taken root, particularly given the shrill, violent and mindless interpretations of many of its loudest and most 'media-friendly' exponents, who are enough to make any decent person look elsewhere for life's deepest meanings. It examines alternative homes for the human spirit and concludes that, after all, there are some things to be said in favour of mainstream religion.

Chapter 2 looks at religion in the Christian West and describes why it is in the difficult state it now finds itself, and how this has impacted the present discipline of religious studies, not always to God's or religion's advantage. Chapter 3 suggests that contemporary western Christians have much to learn from other cultures' ways of being religious. It also argues the case that religion is the means whereby we know God, and is not an end in itself. Even so, we benefit from entering into a creative and disciplined engagement with our religious heritage, rather than from the current self-serving, trivial and rather foolish tendency to make things up as we go along.

Some people have privileged institutional religion, giving greatest weight to what the Pope or the minister or some other ecclesiastical fixture says about matters of faith and belief. Others have conferred authority (instead or as well) upon religion's intellectual traditions, taking careful note of what must be believed, said and done. Organizations and scholarship are two significant dimensions of religion, but their relative importance has often been overestimated. Chapter 4 illustrates my conviction that the heart of religion is God's love for his human children. We see this in the lives and experiences of the mystics, but their intense relationship with transcendent reality is different only in degree and not in kind from that which God desires and hopes to have with all people. Chapter 5 explores truth, and regards it as a quest with God to God. To identify truth solely with factual accuracy or institutional fiats or doctrinal orthodoxy is, to use a phrase beloved by Muslims, manifest error. The final chapter looks at worship and the Bible as resources for the Christian's journey, and asks how they and other spiritual provisions can help us live in faith, hope and love, and prepare us for life's last great adventure of death.

This is not the sort of book that depends upon a battery of complex terminology and endnotes to make its case. I have included endnotes when I want to make an explanatory point or encourage people to read more widely in a book from which

I have quoted or to which I have referred. The bibliography contains many of the works that have helped me form my opinions, in agreement with or in contrast to those of their authors. I have adopted a rather more personal, even anecdotal, style in some places here than in many of my writings. I hope that readers will understand why I have done so, and indulge me. This is not intended to be a book that offers conclusions about one theme and then moves on to another. I revisit topics from time to time in different chapters. I hope that my readers will find that this opens fresh ideas about them from different perspectives. I am under no illusion that this is a book that settles anything, nor is it intended to. It is meant to stimulate thought and action about religion and faith and Christianity and God and other religious issues that humans have always argued passionately about.

These days, writing about God raises interesting gender issues. God has traditionally been held to be without body, parts or passions, though this has not stopped generations of theologians and other believers from using the male pronoun to denote 'him'. I am among those for whom the excessive use of the words 'God' or 'Godself' or their like is not only a tiresome grammatical infelicity but also begs an important theological and liturgical question or two. I raise the importance of how we conceptualize God in a number of places in this book. I use both female and male imagery of God.

I had not intended to write this book, but am very glad that I was encouraged to do so. The English composer Sir Edward Elgar, who was far from the Colonel Blimp imperialist that some unseeing critics portray, wrote of his masterpiece *The Dream of Gerontius*: 'I've written it out of my insidest inside.' Somewhat to my surprise, I find I can say the same about *The Nature and the Name of Love*. I am particularly glad and grateful that it is published by Methodism's press. I shall make some severe criticisms of modern Methodism herein, but roots matter and Methodism's generously inclusive tradition of faith has nourished and supported me since I joined the Church as a teenager almost 40 years ago. I am immeasurably in its debt.

I am also obligated to people of many faiths. I was an Air Force brat, as they say in the part of the world where I now live, travelling the world in my earliest years, which coincided with the closing stages of the British Empire. My first religious memories are of Chinese festivals in Singapore, and my profoundest early experiences were of the diverse worlds of Islam in Aden, now part of Yemen at the heel of the Arabian peninsular. Of all the places that formed me, I am most grateful to India, where I spent two years after theological college, and made Hindu, Muslim, Christian, Sikh, Parsi, Jewish and other friends, with many of whom I stay in touch. Others are now dead, and the memories of their kindness and affection to me, a stranger, fill me with hope for my remaining days on earth. If there is a decisive verse for interfaith dialogue, it is surely Leviticus 19.34, which it is a delight to find in a book that might otherwise be regarded as 'chloroform in print':[1] 'The stranger who resides with you shall be to you as the citizen among you; you shall love the stranger as yourself, for you were strangers in the land of Egypt: I am the LORD your God.'[2] My Indian friends have taught me so much about God's surprisingly inclusive love, despite humankind's besetting sin of drawing boundaries to restrict divine affection to the few. I went to India in the confident hope of a twenty-three-year-old that he was taking God with him and, after an initial jolt and the necessary re-adjustment, was delighted to discover that he was there long before I arrived. This is a book written from the perspective of, and mostly about, Christian faith (though I hope that other religious people will also read it), but it has been crafted out of some knowledge of Islam, Judaism and other worlds of faith, and even more in the context of loving friends from these religions.

As a way of acknowledging the religiously plural world we all inhabit, I refer to CE (Common Era) and BCE (before the

Common Era), rather than BC (before Christ) and AD (*Anno Domini*; the year of the Lord) in the text. To be precise, any dates included herein are assumed to be CE unless I indicate otherwise: so, for example, most scholars believe that Jesus was born about 4 BCE and died around 29 or 30. Candidly, I have never much liked references to CE and BCE, which seem to me to be a patronizing way to secularize and universalize western ways of dating time; I doubt that they make any meaningful contribution to human diversity. Still, until someone finds a better way, this system will have to do.

I was invited to deliver the Teape lectures at St Stephen's College, Delhi, in December 2002. The ideas I first aired there have found their way into this book, though in much changed form. Principal Anil Wilson and his wife Rita were the most gracious of hosts, and I thank them and their colleagues for their hospitality, and former colleagues at Cambridge University for honouring me with the invitation to deliver these prestigious lectures.

I have other specific debts, and am glad to pay them, with the necessary proviso that I cannot and do not want to blame others for my own shortcomings. Michael Townsend suggested to me (and also to others) that I write a book for the Epworth Press, and Ivor Jones and Jonathan Dean, who were then on its Editorial Committee, also led me to believe that I had something to write about. Epworth's Head of Publishing, Natalie Watson, has been a model of patience and encouragement. I have been very fortunate to work at Aurora University for the last six years. I am grateful to its president, Rebecca Sherrick, whose encouragement for and support of the study of religion has made my time here a delight. My past and present colleagues in the university's Wackerlin Center for Faith and Action have been a great source of intellectual stimulus and amusing jokes, and they have mostly stopped me from chasing after my dafter ideas and more harebrained schemes. So I am obliged to Joe Dunham, Gregory Swedberg, Aaron Hendershott, Tim Brauhn and Alex DeGurian. Among other university colleagues, I should mention Richard Westphal, Susan Palmer, Ida Dunham, Michael Moser and Andrew Manion, with thanks for conversations from which I have stolen many good ideas and turned them into my own. I am fortunate to attend New England Congregational Church, and benefit from the good humour and excellent sermons of my pastors there, Gary McCann and (once again) Joe Dunham. Teachers learn a great deal from their students, and I would like especially to thank the firstfruit of the harvest of the university's new Religion major: Drew Taylor, Tim Galvan and Eric Hunt.

Udho has coped with my preoccupied mind while I have been writing this book. Naomi has occasionally taken time out from her tireless and sometimes tiresome vocation of being 17 years old, long enough to enquire how the book is progressing and whether I have finished it. Now that I have, it becomes a small gift to them. In their love and commitment, I see mirrored a large measure of God's, and so to them this book is dedicated, in gratitude and with all my heart.

Has Religion a Future?

God decides to write a letter to a prominent North American evangelist. It runs like this:

> Dear Pat,
> I imagine that you would like me to thank you for your work on my behalf; but actually, no thanks. Why do you divide the world into good and bad, instead of seeing signs of hope even in the most unlikely places? And why does your idea of good seem trivial and even wicked to many who can't go along with you? What's with all this bad temper, partisan politics, and bile? I thought you were supposed to be made in my image, not I in yours. Actually, I'm not paranoid, macho and dumb. You, however, have a way to go. I'm an optimist: you might make it.
> Love,
> God

While God is in epistolary mode, he pens a similar letter to a Muslim member of al-Qaida (to 'Dear Osama', perhaps). He is considering a similar letter to certain Buddhist and Hindu promoters of violence in Sri Lanka, and to some Jewish settlers in occupied territories.

God must get fed up with the self-serving antics of many of his most noisy followers. After all, largely because of them, religion has a bad name among many people in today's world. Its cause is not helped when so many of its members, especially self-appointed and media-hungry leaders, are deficient in humanity, good works, and wisdom.

Has religion run its course?

Our task in this chapter is to explore whether religion has any future at all on earth. The actions of many of its followers are not the only strike against it. Another is the claim that the investigative techniques of modern science render a religious view of life incredible, held only by those who cannot or who will not think straight, or who use it as a prop to hold up their lives, or as an idea to take advantage of the gullible.

We should begin by noting that this scepticism arises out of a particular background: that of Europe (mostly, but not only Western Europe) and, to some extent, the lands Europeans colonized and settled in the modern period. Why Europe has become a post-Christian continent will be discussed in chapter 2. Our emphasis here is that religion flourishes in most of the rest of the world. Sceptics often seem flummoxed about the continuing importance of religion in the USA. They often regard it as an aberration, a hangover from the importance of religion to the early white settlers, and often held by hicks in backward parts of the country. As for the rest of the world, both European and North American media often give a slanted view of religion in 'developing' countries, associating it with people who easily turn to violence, whether in the Middle East, or Sri Lanka, or Central Asia, or Africa, or Indonesia, or some other place or places. This gives the impression that, where religion is alive and well, it is a reactionary and barbaric force, and should be replaced by western-style secular values.

Many Europeans and North Americans display an unexamined condescension towards other parts of the world. They blithely forget or are ignorant of the fact that many of the troubles there were introduced by their forebears, and that 'secular values' could be seen by others both as a contradiction in terms and as the latest self-serving, irrelevant and impertinent imposition upon other cultures. Westerners often imagine the world in relation to their own needs, and not out of any real empathy or even understanding. The designation 'Middle East', for example, was first used to describe and judge West Asia from the viewpoint of Britain's geographical position and colonial history; and the word 'developing' often implies a lower position in understanding things than that afforded to superior persons and cultures.

Sometimes it seems as if it is impossible for Europeans and North Americans to treat people from other cultures, and their faith, in an adult way. Neo-conservatives imagine a clash of civilizations between white and other, particularly Islamic, cultures, and, when given access to political power, advocate and help put into place policies that unnecessarily bring about what they fear and predict. 'Progressives' can be just as imprudent and patronizing. They are among the first to condemn the actions of their own leaders, yet often excuse the words and actions of appalling and wicked religious or political leaders in Asia and Africa on the grounds of some grand post-colonial theory of western guilt and non-western innocence that makes sense only on paper and only to them.

There is a lot of religion in the world outside Europe. Some of its exponents act in bad faith, but many others do not. For many people in the world, religion gives them status and dignity. In fact, to some poor people living under repressive regimes, it is about the only thing that does. This does not, of course, make religion true. But neither does it make it false: hope is, after all, a universal religious quality. Westerners often assume that others would be less religious if they had our western education, democratic values and consumer lifestyle, but they could be wrong. Many people who reject the secular values of the West have tried and abandoned its hedonistic lifestyle but embrace its technology to further their ends: members of al-Qaida, for example, who use the world-wide web to keep in touch with each other and to horrify others by telling of their plans and putting up photographs of their deeds. Even if westerners are not wrong, and secularism will inevitably if slowly spell the end of religion, that could be a pity, for western civilization might not be a good model for others to follow (look, for example, at its rampant selfishness and greed, which most religions' core teachings abhor). If we wish to understand the world in which we live, we would do well to listen to other voices of faith from around the world. Then, those who think that they have outgrown religion might discover from some of them that their diminished and limited understanding of it means that they have not understood how it can speak words of grace and glory.

We have to give some persuasive definition of religion before we can assess its future, whether globally or in Europe, North America or some other region. Religion is rather a slippery word. For our purposes, let it stand for two things. The first is a structured system of belief, thought and action, such as Buddhism, Christianity and Islam. We talk of the Buddhist religion; the Christian religion; and the religion of Islam. The second is faith in what some people call God. Others call it or him or her or them by another name or names because they have a different way of conceptualizing and indicating a transcendent dimension to life; a dimension that makes its presence felt in ordinary human affairs to those who have the wisdom (or, its critics would say, are gullible enough) to believe in its power and act upon that belief.

For the moment, let us pause before this second interpretation of religion. Mystics see this God-dimension of life very clearly indeed. The nineteenth-century Anglican clergyman John Keble describes it in a hymn that is still sung today (it is found, for example, in *Hymns & Psalms* 340):

Two worlds are ours: 'tis only sin
Forbids us to descry
The mystic heaven and earth within,
Plain as the sea and sky.

Thou who hast given me eyes to see
And love this sight so fair,
Give me a heart to find out thee,
And read thee everywhere.

A secular person would not agree with these sentiments. The word 'secular' comes from a Latin word that has a range of meanings. It can mean 'worldly' or 'pagan'. Sometimes it refers to the 'laity' rather than the clergy. It has come to be used, in a sense derived from these meanings, to denote a humanist, non-religious view of reality: what is real is what we can see, or descry with our senses, or deduce on the basis of empirical evidence or scientific data. Not only is there no afterlife, however defined by whatever religious or philosophical traditions, but also the world is not troubled by the attentions of any transcendent presence.

Secularists find it impossible to believe in a world that is open to God's presence; or so we often read. In fact, things may not be as simple as that, because most people's secularism is not that rigorous. Although almost every European and North American is influenced by secularism, as are millions more around the world, it has not destroyed the human obsession with religion. Over 70 years of communism in Russia did not destroy religion, and 60 years of communism in China have not eradicated religion there. After the Second World War until 1990, the communist Albanian government cracked down hard on religion (which is mostly Islam there), but now over 25 per cent of the population take part in formal religious acts.

To be sure, in the contemporary world and particularly in Europe, there are plenty of atheists: people who deny the existence of God. The strength and passion of their denial often gives the impression that some of them are at least as fixated on religion as are many people of faith. Many unbelievers hold that the idea of God, which has no basis in reason, has wreaked havoc and violence on the world, and should be abandoned as a dangerous delusion. For example, books by the Oxford scientist Richard Dawkins that market these ideas sell very well indeed; not least *The God Delusion*. In 2007, Dawkins was chosen by *Time* magazine as one of the hundred most influential people in the world. Even so, it is rather telling that someone who holds an Oxford University Chair in the Public Understanding of Science should interpret it to mean the public denigration of religion, and intriguing that that ancient university thinks that it is an appropriate academic enterprise for him to do so. One could make the case that his is a public misunderstanding of religion, for Dawkins's views provide an excellent example of unexamined, modernist assumptions about the nature of religion[1] and its relationship with science, formed within a narrow Eurocentric view of the world and of intellectual thought. Science and religion have not always been antagonistic towards each other; for example, in medieval Muslim cultures there was a harmonious and creative interaction between the two.[2]

In point of fact, it is not too hard to criticize Dawkins' work. At one level, he is an unabashed polemicist, which makes *The God Delusion* fun to read but hard to take seriously. He follows the devices and desires of many controversialists. He has a list of targets whom, in aiming at and mocking, he fails to assess fairly or seriously. These include theologians ancient and modern, like Thomas Aquinas and Richard Swinburne; and the Templeton Foundation, whose aim it is to bring science and religion together in fruitful ways of which Dawkins cannot approve. He presents his own side at its best (there is not much in his work about the link between scientific research and technology put to destructive and harmful ends), and his opponents' positions at their worst, so that the reader has the impression that 'religion poisons everything'.[3] The superficiality of many of his philosophical judgements could be seen by any intelligent undergraduate, and he has little or no sense of the discipline of history and its insights about the constraints upon and possibilities open to people in different times and places. He laments how ill-used atheists are in a world dominated by religion, a complaint that has some force in the USA, rather more in some Islamic countries, but not much in secular Britain (where he lives) and Europe where, it could as easily be asserted, religious people are regarded as strange and aberrant (not least by people like himself). He has a tendency to interpret people whom he admires, but whose views do not apparently agree with his own, to mean what he wants them to mean, even when they claim otherwise. So, for example, he does not believe that Albert Einstein's commitment to religion was really to religion at all. Rather, the great man held Einsteinian 'religion', free from theistic belief and actually as atheistic as Dawkins' own beliefs. As we shall shortly see, Einstein's religious views were certainly eccentric but Dawkins fails to interpret them as carefully as Einstein himself does. He would do well carefully to examine Einstein's comment that: 'There are people who say that there is no God. But what makes me really angry is that they quote me in support of such views.'[4]

Unlike Einstein, Dawkins is not much interested in, perhaps not even aware of, the complexities of religion. Not for him any serious reflection on the multi-dimensional nature of religion, which any student in an introductory class on the subject would have to understand in order to pass it. His assertion that 'the existence of God is a scientific hypothesis like any other'[5] illustrates his tendency to interpret complex phenomena and data over-simplistically through a single lens of human thought and experience. He also makes religion mean, for all practical purposes, the Abrahamic faiths of Judaism, Christianity and Islam. By a process of reducing these faiths to a partial and superficial reading of their sacred texts, he interprets them as portraying a bad-tempered, violent, destructive and interventionist super-natural being, much like the one believed in by the Pat and the Osama to whom, at the beginning of this chapter, I imagined God writing letters of rebuke and disavowal. Ironically, extreme partisans who define their position in a one-dimensional way often look to others to have more in common with each other than they think, far more than they have with many ordinary believers and unbelievers.

Dawkins thinks that religion offers up trivial beliefs that can be easily refuted. Yet we have already encountered two related but different interpretations of religion, systems of faith and a belief in transcendent reality, and each of these is a complex web of related things. Think for example of the Hindu religion and how varied it is: some Hindus believe in a personal god whereas others do not; some worship the mother goddess, while others are repelled by this devotion but find comfort and hope in some of its sacred writings; and so on. Multi-faceted religious systems and myriad forms of reflecting upon and depicting the nature of transcendent reality should not be made into a straw man that can easily be destroyed. Dawkins writes:

> Imagine, with John Lennon, a world with no religion. Imagine no suicide bombers, no 9/11, no Crusades, no witch-hunts, no Gunpowder Plot, no Indian partition, no Israeli–Palestinian wars, no Serb/Croat/Muslim massacres, no persecution of Jews as 'Christ-killers', no Northern Ireland 'troubles', no 'honour killings', no shiny-suited bouffant-haired televangelists fleecing gullible people of their money ('God wants you to give till it hurts').[6]

This is amusing, knock-about stuff, though, if Dawkins sincerely thinks that belief in God is the sole or even major cause of all these things, he shows an out-of-touch naïveté outstanding even in an Oxford professor. He has not followed truth wherever it may lead: in this case, to where religion becomes entangled, for good and for ill, in politics, economics, the pursuit of power and other human enterprises. Moreover, to attack religions on the grounds that, for example, they caused the events of 11 September 2001 or 7 July 2005 is to overlook their teachings of peace and justice, and the quality of life displayed by many people over many centuries who have appropriated and lived them out. It is also to fail to acknowledge that many pious Muslims and other people of faith are appalled by the hijacking of religion by wicked people in the name of a violent God.

For Dawkins, religion is, at bottom, superstitious belief in a personal God who interferes in this world in ways that he and others believe science has shown not to be possible. He caricatures believers as people who are mostly either morally or intellectually challenged. He is blind to the compelling power of religion for most people in most times and places. Most especially, he misses the note of mystery and wonder that comes to many people, not just from contemplating the workings of the human body or the Milky Way or some other scientifically respectable phenomenon, but from a sense that all these may be a small part of a wonderful and loving process in which they and all things are caught up. Such people may be wrong, but they are not necessarily bad-tempered, perverse and stupid.

Dawkins' critique of religion puts one in mind of a tone-deaf person consigning Bach, Beethoven, Brahms and the Beatles to the dustbin of musical and cultural history. The criticisms that hit home could be made just as severely but with more nuance, irony and admiration, and more fittingly, by those who appreciate genius but do not feel compelled to fawn or pass over its areas of darkness. Religion is more likely to reveal its secrets to those who wield a rapier wit and wisdom than those who carry a bludgeon. In fact, it is likely that Dawkins' work will eventually be revealed as inadequate and somewhat old-fashioned, not just by religionists but also by scientists who doubt whether the complexities of their work and its contribution to the story of humankind can be adequately confined to the restrictive biological model of scientific investigation with which he operates.

A compelling, fair-minded and reasonable case can be made that, on balance, religions do not promote human welfare, and that the transcendent reality to which they point and witness is unreal. However, it is an unfortunate characteristic of many contemporary critics of religion to point only to its shady side. Why would you read Christian behaviour from members of the Ku Klux Klan when you can do so from quite ordinary church members who try to do good and make the world a better place? Or why understand Muslim attitudes from al-Qaida when you might be captivated by the humane and compassionate views that shaped the creation of the Red Crescent Society, which works to help and to heal? Is Mahatma Gandhi less compelling and mainstream a spokesperson for his religion than the Hindu who killed him?

It seems a shame that some critics of religion cannot understand its alluring power over most people of the past and the present. It is even more foolish when they distort and trivialize religion in order to dismiss it. Religion has, among many other things, shaped art and architecture, formed great thinkers, provided wonderful stories that have transformed people's lives for good, inspired the creation of national laws and institutions. It deserves to be taken seriously, even, perhaps especially, when some or all of its core convictions are rejected.

Moreover, some secularists are blithely untroubled by the catastrophic effects of many unbelievers on the twentieth-century world: Stalin, Hitler, Mao, Pol Pot are among the irreligious monsters who utilized technology to wreak havoc and devastation on millions of innocent people. Some critics of religious worldviews have attempted to make the case that fascism and communism are varieties of religion, or some such specious and unworthy argument. Another recent neo-atheist critic of religion, Christopher Hitchens, referring to the Hitler and Stalin regimes, tells us that they 'show us with terrible clarity what can happen when men usurp the role of gods'.[7] The Nazi and Stalinist regimes were secular, whose leaders used religion cynically, when at all. Hitchens' act of unquiet desperation illustrates that it is impossible to persuade such unreasonable polemicists of a more positive view of humankind's many ways of faith, or to subject their own secular views to a measure of self-evaluation and self-criticism.

The idea of God and many other aspects of religion should be considered thoughtfully, for they have been long and deeply rooted in human civilization. On the other hand, many of religion's most vocal partisans should not be taken as seriously by others as they take themselves. They often have as trivial a view of religion as some of its recent critics, and deserve the censure of many. No doubt Dawkins and other such writers (recent American counterparts would be Sam Harris, who has written a *Letter to a Christian Nation*, and the aforementioned Christopher Hitchens, the title of whose book *God Is Not Great* seems to be a deliberate mockery of Islam's central belief that God is greater than anything else that can be named) appeal, not just to diehard atheists but to many people of goodwill whose negative views of religion are shaped by the unappealing, divisive and sometimes violent certainties of some of its vociferous proponents. The media introduce us to such bad-tempered, even vicious religious people every day.

Alas, it is not just mad and bad exponents of religion who give it a bad name: some mainstream religious people, including faith leaders, do not seem to realize or even care about the negative impressions they make upon other people, including those of goodwill. Take, for example, the Church of England's and its sister churches' divisions about homosexuality, which have brought them to the brink of schism. Outsiders could be forgiven for wondering what on earth this is all about. Surely there are more important things to talk about, like justice and the integrity of creation, or even the abuse of any form of human sexual identity; things, indeed, that are more grounded in Scripture than particular attitudes towards human sexuality, even though many of those who are obsessed by this issue claim to be Bible-based Christians.

As another example, in the USA many so-called 'born again' Christians believe that we are living in the end times. This means that large numbers of them are indifferent to environmental issues: why bother to cherish the earth if it is shortly to be destroyed or otherwise radically transformed by God? They also have bizarre convictions about the need for Jews to return to the Holy Land in great numbers before Jesus returns again, where Armageddon is to take place (soon, in the view of many of them). Such muddled, imprudent, eccentric, contrived and daft biblical interpretation hinders some politicians from taking actions that would sustain our planet, and from promoting a sensible, just and lasting peace in the Middle East.[8]

Some people who hold such imprudent views are intelligent and charming. Hanna Rosin, a Jewish author, recently wrote a book about Patrick Henry College, a small college just outside Washington D.C., which attempts to produce graduates who will become important politicians, judges and other people who can, in their view, save America by reintroducing their brand of Christian values. Quite a few of its students provided internees for the Bush White House and Congress. One student lodged with Rosin, and became close to the family and they to her. One day Rosin's husband asked her: '"So, are we going to Hell?" . . . "Yes," she answered. "But I'm not jumping up and down with joy about it."'[9] I am not as sure as once I was that people are entitled to their own views. Vicious and exclusive views are still vicious and exclusive, however charmingly held. They lead some to think that God really does share their views. And if the plan of people who hold them is to gain the power to impose them on others, other Christians should surely confront them with more Christ-like values. I was once reading a book in the grounds of Westcott College, Cambridge, when an American tourist wandered in with a T-shirt that read 'Jesus would vote Republican'. I thought: what makes you think that? And how do you know? On reflection, I should have challenged him instead of carrying on reading.

Examples like these seem to reinforce the assertions of Dawkins and others that religion is a menace, an impediment to human flourishing. No wonder he writes best-sellers. Yet it is intriguing that although some people are turned off by religion, they do not feel comfortable with Dawkins' austere commitment to his particular view of science as revealing all that we can know of life's meanings. Maybe this discomfort is because they intuit that Dawkins' position replaces one unconvincing interpretation of the universe with another. Religious and secular fundamentalists alike reduce the mysteries of life to manageable and, truth to tell, trivial 'certainties'. Unlike St Paul, they have no sense that 'now I know only in part' (1 Corinthians 13.12). They lack humility.

The great scientist Albert Einstein is a wise guide in this matter. He wrote in a letter: 'What separates me from most so-called atheists is a feeling of utter humility towards the unattainable secrets of the harmony of the cosmos.'[10] The conclusion of a speech that he gave on the relationship between science and religion at the Union Theological Seminary in New York was: 'The situation may be expressed by an image: science without religion is lame, religion without science is blind.'[11] Einstein could not be counted an Orthodox Jew in any meaningful sense. He was a determinist, which would logically remove him from the view of most Jewish and Christian theologians that people are responsible for their actions. Nor did he believe in a personal God: he supposed that this requires trust in a cosmic force that intervenes in creation and disrupts the immutable laws that govern (and determine) reality. He did not accept as true any future life for an individual, either in heaven or else reincarnated on earth. Still, the point is not about whether or not Einstein was a mainstream religious believer or thinker. Clearly, he was not. Rather, it is to point to his sense of awe in the face of the universe's mysteriousness, grounded, not just in scientific knowledge, but in the humane (and human) possibilities of love, joy, hope, repentance and their like. Einstein wrote:

> The most beautiful emotion we can experience is the mysterious. It is the fundamental emotion that stands at the cradle of all true art and science. He to whom this emotion is a stranger, who can no longer wonder and stand rapt in awe, is as good as dead, a snuffed-out candle. To sense that behind anything that can be experienced there is something that our minds cannot grasp, whose beauty and sublimity reaches us only indirectly: this is religiousness. In this sense, and in this sense only, I am a devoutly religious man.[12]

Many noisy religious people and many loquacious secularists have in common a rather simplistic view of the world and how it fundamentally is. Members of the former group believe that a bad-tempered and socio-pathological deity, who sometimes displays their own traits, governs the world, or would do if only 'wicked' people (those of whom they disapprove) were removed. The latter group includes those who interpret the world with an equally aggressive assurance that the little they can figure out about it is all that matters, views that they often hold with as much bad temper, or at least petulance and arrogance, as religious fundamentalists. Where, one wonders, are the mystery, wonder, awe and reverence that characterize, not just good religion and good science, but decent human beings who have a sense of proportion and whose good acts arise from decent convictions?

If not religion or secularism, then what?

Lots of people are, like Einstein, unconventional believers who have a reverent attitude towards the nature of reality. Many of them find the teachings and practices of religion to be unlikable or unbelievable, yet still hanker after a sense of mystery and wonder that cannot be proven by Dawkins' restrictive criteria. Such people will often say something along the lines of: 'I'm not religious, but I'm very spiritual.' What they often mean by this is that they do not attend church or mosque or synagogue or some other house of worship, but reckon that their lives have some positive, often ethical quality about them. Occasionally, hearers are tempted to retort, 'I'll be the judge of that.' Still, that sometimes rather defensive and glib comment of 'very spiritual' persons suggests that it is not just (or even) belief in God that is problematic for them. Religions may have gone sour on them, but neither can they buy into the certainty of strict secularists that following empirical evidence to its conclusions offers all possible answers to the questions life poses.

So the issue arises: if not religion and if not secularism, then what? Many people are put off by zealots for secular values or for their religion, who seem arrogantly confident in their certainties. Some secularists take it for granted that, as western science, technology and values spread across the globe, these will inevitably sound the death-knell for religion. But they can only hold this presupposition if they are parochially Euro-centric and either do not notice resurgent religion across much of the rest of the world or are just puzzled by it and put it down to (hopefully) temporary fanaticism. Equally ardent exponents of religious faith often assume that the form in which they know it will last for ever and ever, but, to steal a line from George Gershwin, 'it ain't necessarily so'. It ain't even usually so: one of the longest lasting of all religions was the ancient Egyptian faith, lasting from at least as early as the building of the pyramids at Giza around 2600 BCE until about the fourth century CE; but now it is as dead as the dodo. Our faith may tell us that our Jewish, or Christian, or Muslim, or Hindu, or Buddhist religion is here to stay, but it may be misplaced faith; misplaced because, as we shall see later in this book, religions are means and not ends and are intended to have a finite conclusion; and also because if they stop conveying to their believers a compelling vision of reality, people abandon them. History is littered with the remains of once-popular religions. Even so, the force that created and sustained them endures. If you followed the ancient Egyptian faith in Alexandria in the second century of the Common Era, and saw your traditional beliefs and faith-structures crumbling around you, that might make you brood over whether God is dead or dying; but in fact your descendants a couple of centuries later would be worshipping him as Coptic Christians, and some of their descendants a few centuries later would be saying their prayers to Allah.

A secular person, noting this, could argue that she is right to claim that, taking the long view, religions are passing phenomena. Even the ones that last change their shape and even some of their core convictions over time and space. But that argument is to miss the point. Religions wax and wane, but belief in transcendent reality is an enduring human characteristic. An austerely logical assessment of religion could lead to the conclusion that it is wiser to ask what sort of religion we should have, rather than whether there should be religion at all. Religion is, after all, an abiding human preoccupation, dating back to prehistoric times. Evidence from prehistoric times suggests that humans believed in mysteries beyond the capacity of their eyes to scan, including maybe even belief in an afterlife: for example, red ochre was used to stain bones in some Neanderthal burial grounds about 150,000 years ago, probably for ritual purposes. Cave paintings at Lascaux (*c.* 15,000 BCE) and at Arièges (*c.* 12,000–11,000 BCE), both in modern France, seem to indicate reverence for the world around the artists, and may have been part of a relatively complex system of rites. Certainly, what we would nowadays recognize as religious systems were emerging by about 3000 BCE in Egypt, Iraq and China. Religion is a very, very longstanding human enterprise and commitment.

It should not surprise us, therefore, to find that most people in the contemporary West continue to be gripped by religion. When religions fail, secularism does not inevitably take over. If the religion we have had most to do with (whether we were born into it or because it is the primary one in our setting, or for some other reason) loses its fascination, and if the secular alternative does not work for us, then we are spoiled for choice. We can choose another one. There are many religious alternatives on offer. So Jews become Buddhists, Christians become Muslims, and so on. And vice versa, of course: members of religions who trumpet abroad the numbers of their converts are not usually given to passing on information about their own adherents who leave for another faith.

It is often easy to make guesses about why people choose another religion than their own. They may feel that their original faith demeans their sex or sexuality, their ethnicity or some other intrinsic part of them. They may marry a person of another religion, and think that it is easier to embrace (most usually) his religion than maintain their own. They may hanker after a religion that has, in their view, more clear-cut opinions, or even truths, to tell about things. Or they may want a more tolerant faith by which to steer their life. Some surveys of why people change their faith give the impression of seeking one major reason, and this is often the case. In talking with people who make such a life-changing move from one faith to another, you will indeed often find that there is a dominant reason. Sometimes, however, the secondary reasons prove as interesting and important as the major one. A woman who converts on marriage from, say, Christianity to Islam, may find that a decision taken on pragmatic grounds becomes one that, slowly but surely, she can embrace joyfully on the grounds of genuine faith and belief. Or she may gradually find that she never fully feels at home and that some irreducible element or elements of Christianity remain part of the core of her being.

A sideways move into another world religion is not the only possibility open to today's spiritual seekers. There seem to be endless alternative ways of faith out there, and reasons for choosing them are often (but not always) the same as or very similar to those adduced for removing to another mainstream religion. We mention, broadly, only two of these alternative spiritualities.

Alternatives to mainstream religions:
1 New Religious Movements

The first is New Religious Movements (NRMs). There are a great many of them. A list of those that begin with the first letter of the alphabet would include: Adidam; Ananda Church of Self-Realization; Ananda Marga Yoga Society; Aetherius Society; Association for Research and Enlightenment; Aum Shinrikyo (now called Aleph). As the designation NRM indicates, these groups are relatively recent foundations, though some of them have emerged out of Hinduism, Christianity or some other longstanding world religion and draw upon aspects of its teaching, usually in new, unusual and sometimes almost unrecognizable ways.

They are held in suspicion by many outsiders, not least by those from whose religion they spring. Sometimes this suspicion is justified. Take, as examples, the fate of the Peoples Temple Christian Church, and the activities of Aum Shinrikyo.

The Peoples Temple Christian Church was founded by Jim Jones in 1956. In 1960 it became part of the Disciples of Christ denomination. Jones, however, was no exponent of mainstream Christian belief, rejecting the Bible on the grounds that 'the letter killeth'. The movement moved west from Indianapolis to California. For a while, Jones' followers did much good work, not least in a poor district of San Francisco. In 1974, he bought land in Guyana, South America, to develop about 4,000 acres in the northwest part of the country. When the US Inland Revenue Service began to look closely at the Temple's income in the spring of 1977, around the time when former members were expressing their disaffection with Jones and his group, he encouraged US members to move to his holding in Guyana. About 1,000 did so, to a settlement that became known as Jonestown. In November 1978, California Congressman Ryan went on a fact-finding expedition to Jonestown. As he was preparing to leave there with some defecting members, he was shot dead by Jones' followers, along with one Temple member and three journalists; others were seriously injured. As a result, Jones persuaded most of his remaining followers that 'revolutionary suicide' was their only option, though he had to intimidate a few. He was killed with a gunshot wound in his head, and the others died of a cyanide cocktail. Over 900 people died, children first, with some mothers forcing the drink down their children's throats. It was the largest mass suicide (or maybe murder is the better designation) in US history.

Aum Shinrikyo was founded in 1986 by Asaharo Shoko (b. 1955). It began as a Japanese meditation group, teaching what Asaharo saw as the truth about the creation and destruction of the universe. Asaharo had visited India in 1986 (where he changed his name from Chizuo Matsumoto), and came to believe that meditation removes bad karma. He also believed that suffering promoted good karma, and soon there were claims of the abuse of others. His works contain a mixture of Buddhist, Hindu and Taoist ideas, with an emphasis on the veneration of Shiva as lord of destruction. Indeed, as time went by, his sermons and publications had a stronger apocalyptic focus drawn not just from Hindu but also from Christian thought, specifically the New Testament book of Revelation. In 1989, Asaharo founded a political party, and in 1994 set himself up as an alternative government to the elected Japanese one. By then, he had stopped trying to prevent an apocalypse and was more concerned to rescue his followers from the one he felt was certainly at hand. For some time, he had made a number of moves against his 'enemies' and others. For example, in 1989, a

Yokohama lawyer with experience of NRMs was hired by ex-members, and began to move against Aum Shinrikyo. In November that year, he disappeared with his wife and son; their bodies were found in 1995. Asaharo's most notorious command to followers was obeyed on 20 March 1995. In the midst of the morning rush hour, ten highly placed members boarded five trains at different stations. As they left their trains, they punctured with umbrellas bags of sarin wrapped in newspaper. The Kasumigaseki Station suffered the worst of the attack. The time and place appear to have been deliberately selected, as Kasumigaseki Station is located under many government offices and the National Police Agency's headquarters. Twelve people died and thousands were incapacitated in this March gassing. A series of indictments followed. Asaharo himself was arraigned for:

- murder, in relation to the Tokyo sarin gas attack on 20 March 1995
- murder, in relation to the Matsumoto Nagano Prefecture sarin gas attack in June 1994 (seven killed and 600 injured)
- the kidnapping and murder of Tsutsumi Sakamoto (the Yokohama lawyer representing Aum member parents) and his wife and infant son
- the kidnapping and death of Kiyoshi Kariya (a Tokyo notary public) in February 1995
- the lynching of Kotata Ochida (an 'uncooperative' Aum member) in February 1994
- the illegal production of various drugs.

Under different leadership, Aum Shinrikyo has regrouped and changed its name to Aleph, which means to start anew. This fresh beginning has not so far included any desire to condemn outright Asaharo's beliefs and deeds.

Such attention-grabbing activities as those of Jones' and Asaharo's organizations mean that it is hardly surprising that

NRMs are regarded with suspicion by many people. They are often referred to as cults, a word that, for many people, has sinister and negative connotations. It has become easy to denigrate them all. Yet each NRM has its own characteristics, and most are more counter-cultural than anti-social. They offer (often young) people an alternative to what they see as the economically affluent but morally and spiritually bankrupt society around them.

Although each NRM is different, certain distinguishing features mark out many of them. NRMs frequently have authoritarian leaders, who insist upon being obeyed absolutely. Members often have to be initiated into the group, and are discouraged from leaving, though most do. Quite often NRMs have relatively few followers, but make an impact out of all proportion to their numbers. Because adolescents and young adults are often attracted to NRMs, this leads to accusations that they have been brainwashed at a vulnerable time in their lives. Some NRMs are (or seem to intelligent observers to be) all about money, power and sex. Many NRM founders and leaders are very well off indeed, and exercise considerable control over their 'flock'. Not only are some leaders (like Jim Jones) sexually predatory; they will also use sex to gain converts. For example, from 1974 to 1987, the Children of God movement, based in Huntington Beach, California, used 'flirty fishing' as a form of religious prostitution to bait converts. Women members were told to be 'God's whores' and 'hookers for Jesus'. Members envisaged Jesus having sex with them during sex and masturbation, and male members had to imagine themselves as women, in order to ensure that this was not a homosexual activity. Not just the movement but also David Berg, its founder who died in 1994, did well financially from this form of religious pandering.

However, not all NRMs are run by wicked, rapacious, delusional or crazy people. It would be better for their critics to work out a nuanced and balanced approach to NRMs, rather than to condemn them all out of hand. A significant number of people who join them are educated and thoughtful, who cannot easily be accused of having been brainwashed. Many NRMs hold unusual views, sometimes drawn eccentrically from Christianity or some other mainstream religion's convictions, but this does not necessarily make them depraved organizations. After all, every major religion was a new religious movement when it began, and was often held in suspicion by the group it hoped to co-exist with or even to supersede. For example, Christianity was originally a small, new Jewish movement (or cult; or sect, another putdown word) that was believed by most Jews to have wrong views about who was the Messiah, and about how non-Jews could correctly become part of God's covenantal promises.

It is helpful and vital to explore reasons why people join NRMs. While it is never a bad idea to criticize the shortcomings of one's own faith (a certain rabbi is held to have once said, humorously, that 'It doesn't matter what religion you belong to, as long as you're ashamed of it'), most sensible people do not join an organization primarily to spite another one. We should examine and admit the strengths of NRMs, and their attractiveness to some. Many have a clear idea of what they believe, and a structure that enables people to know where they stand in its belief-system and also its hierarchy and what is expected of them to progress spiritually (and sometimes materially). So they often appeal to people who value certainty and security in a changing world. They also make demands of them, not just in terms of time and money, but in surrendering their whole lives to a cause. Many young adults join NRMs because they hanker after a spiritual dimension to life, having been brought up by secular parents who have little or nothing to do with religion, or who see it as a convenience or a low-level hobby rather than a lifetime's commitment and challenge. NRMs sometimes abuse those who join them. But groups within mainstream religions and secular organizations do this too. NRMs are often an intriguing blend of East and West, creations of our rapidly globalizing world, appealing to those who are captivated by ideas that are unlike those of their own culture. If they are often superficial, that means that they can be easily assimilated by young people who, in rebellion against what they know, may be inclined to over-sentimentalize their idea of the moment. Moreover, nowadays many young people in secular societies grow up thinking that they have a right to instant gratification.

Some NRMs, with ideas about the importance of unidentified flying objects, gods walking the earth today, and a pile of other eccentric beliefs, can seem crazy, until you reflect that the mainstream teaching of most religions is not obviously true to outsiders, to whom it may seem downright daft. It is important to know that most members of NRMs leave them, and move on to something else or simply fall back into what they have always known and assumed to be true about things. But some stay, convinced by their compelling power or just because they have found friendship and acceptance.

Alternatives to mainstream religions:
2 New Age Movements

NRMs typically appeal to people who look to exterior guidance for their spiritual experience. Traditional authorities like Scripture, clergy or even a self-revealing God may not work for them, but they retain the impulse to seek some kind of outside help. The New Age Movements (NAMs; it is far more exact to refer to movements than to a movement, as many do) cater for rather a different clientele, and appeal to a different impulse.

There is no one focus of authority for new agers. Indeed, the notion that there is some kind of exterior help, whether from God or an authoritative and self-appointed human, puts most of them off. Rather, NAMs provide spiritualities for individuals who are more interested in their self-fulfilment than in self-improvement. Individuals can draw upon aspects of ancient Egyptian religion, Buddhism or Hinduism, or all three and more also in order to achieve this realization. Shamanism, paganism and the occult can also be utilized to construct meaning or meanings in a person's life. Some new agers stroke crystals or embrace alternative medicine or channel spirits or are ardent environmentalists who seek the wellbeing of mother earth. Some practise white magic or astrology or alchemy. As John Drane puts it, 'understanding the New Age is like trying to wrestle with a jelly', precisely because it is amorphous and eclectic in nature, drawing into itself so many new developments like quantum physics, as well as a range of ancient patterns and thoughts, and the mystical elements of many religions: 'Anything and everything that has potential for promoting a change of thinking among the world's people will be sucked up and utilized as we move relentlessly towards the Age of Aquarius.'[13]

In reality, these movements are of relatively recent origin, becoming popular in the 1960s and afterwards, in centres like Findhorn, Scotland, and Glastonbury, England, though they seek validation from a bewildering number of ancient spiritual sources. Despite the individualism and eclecticism and vagueness of NAMs, certain common features can be distinguished through the mist. The Age of Aquarius will be an age of the water-bearer, symbolizing healing and restoration, much needed after the current Age of Pisces in which we now live, the age of the fish. The Piscean Age began with the coming of Jesus and has been characterized by division, conflict, war, injustice, hatred and bigotry, which are all the result of organized religion, dividing God from humankind. Most new agers do not believe in a creator God; indeed, many believe that they are part of God, as are all things. The earth is often depicted as our mother, and we should accept our link to her along with all else, and so protect and not exploit her. All things should work in a harmonious balance: spirituality and science are complementary not antagonistic. Although people and, indeed, all things are inter-connected, so that it is possible to learn from others things that will help us on our life's journey, it is not just a person's right to select from the smorgasbord of spiritual possibilities that which delights and nourishes them, but it is also a responsibility. For most new agers, there is no external reality outside oneself, so you create your own reality.

Many criticisms can and should be made of NAMs. Their anti-intellectualism often goes hand in hand with a naïve assumption that a moment's thought can understand quantum physics, the teachings and history of a major world religion, or some other discipline that can then be easily appropriated in an individualistic way. Most other people believe that such pursuits take considerable effort and patience to master, and a measure of humility before the facts. Severe critics have noted that there is nothing much new about the new age: it is a rehash of old superstitions, badly learned and superficially applied. To be sure, many new agers are relatively prosperous middle-class individuals who desire a therapeutic spirituality that makes few demands upon them but makes them feel good about themselves. Their eclecticism often reveals a superficial knowledge of what they steal and how they interpret it. Many do not realize the offence they offer thereby (for example, to Native Americans by the easy way they imitate sweat lodge ceremonies), or are not troubled by it because spirituality is an individual thing and not about others.

It is natural that members of mainstream religions should disapprove of the NAMs' often undemanding and facile spiritualities, and their emphasis upon an individualism that encourages self-absorption and can justify bad habits like drug-abuse as part of the search for authentic experience. They should, however, reflect that there are not a few Christians, Muslims, Hindus and others whose religion is mostly trivial and self-centred. Furthermore, most new agers seem to be searching for a depth to life (even if, ironically, in shallow ways) that cannot be found when religions grow too rigid and bureaucratic, and exclude others by patriarchy or some other form of elitism that spuriously invokes the divine as its justification. Nor can it be found in a secularism that delights only in materialism, or which finds meaning in a narrow understanding of reason, so that what you see or can prove is all you can know. The new age emphasis upon spontaneity, intuition, wholeness, care for the earth, and personal fulfilment may, to outsiders, seem naïvely and inappropriately expressed, but these are valuable things and not to be despised or forbidden.

Whether paganism should be regarded as an NAM is a vexed question. Some members of NAMs dabble in pagan practices, but many pagans resist the notion that they are new agers. Pagans are often presumed to practise magic and witchcraft, and to deal with the occult. However, many of them point out that pagans have nothing to do with the occult, or practise only good magic. 'Paganism' comes from a word linking devotees to the land: it probably means 'country dweller', though there has been some dispute about this, and it may indicate 'people of the place', who preserved local traditions.

Christians have used 'pagan' (or its equivalent, 'heathen', which derives from an Old English word) to disparage those who have resisted the claims of their religion. They even referred to Muslims in the High Middle Ages as 'paynim', though it was bizarre to describe that monotheistic and originally desert religion by a word that denotes rural settings and rituals. 'Pagan' has been used of atheists and those who live solely for the pleasures of the flesh, especially gluttons. It has sometimes been employed within a family of faith to condemn one or more branches of it: Protestants have accused Catholic and Eastern Orthodox Christians of being pagans, because of their veneration of the saints in paintings, statues or icons. It has been used by missionaries and agents of colonial powers to condemn Hinduism, Buddhism and other religions.

However, the word 'pagan' is nowadays most often used of

pre-Christian European traditions, some of which (like the mid-winter celebration of what became Christmas) were absorbed into the new religion of Christianity. Few contemporary European pagans would claim that they are living out a religion that has survived two millennia of Christian supersessionism. Rather, they create a contemporary re-formation of the themes that marked out pagans of old. They empathize with those who once lived close to the land, to a world of spirit and spirits, to the rhythm of nature and her seasons. In that sense, paganism can be identified with original, primal faith.

Indeed, the concept of paganism has been used of indigenous folk-religion everywhere and, if this usage is allowed, then it can be claimed that paganism is truly a world religion, incorporating the primal faiths of Africa, Siberia, North America and many more places.[14] In some of these places, paganism is the usual form of believing and behaving, or was until recently (for example, in parts of sub-Saharan Africa). Even where they have converted to another religion, many indigenous peoples incorporate pagan rites, practices and values into the faith that has replaced their ancestral beliefs, usually Christianity or Islam.

Whether paganism can meaningfully serve as the term to describe world-wide practices and customs of indigenous or 'first' peoples, and whether it would be important for it (or some other word) to do so, and whether paganism could even be granted the status of a world religion, are questions that cannot easily be resolved: the jury is still out on them. Maybe the verdict will eventually be 'yes, to all of these'; but few outsiders would put money on it. We are not dealing with a set of convictions, however vaguely defined, that can easily be summarized and integrated into a meaningful whole. 'Pagan' can be used of a Japanese man engaged in Shinto practices, and of an African woman telling tales of how the high God of her tribe disappeared into the sky so that now we deal with one or more of many different gods, and of the young woman at the end of your road who has a cat, a pentacle and a cauldron. It can be spoken of by some people in positive ways and by others disparagingly. It could credibly be argued that the word 'pagan' is just a term of insult and putdown, or else that it refers to so wide a group of customs and practices as to be meaningless.

It is interesting and moderately profitable to speculate about how to define NRMs and NAMs (and paganism, if it is to be held as distinct from NAMs). But that is not really the point about them, which is, rather, that they offer distinctive spiritual alternatives to mainstream religious belief; certainly to the Christian religion, which has been the dominant faith of Europe and the Americas. It is not just secularism to which people can turn, if in revolt from the religion of their birth or the dominant faith of the surrounding culture. Intriguingly, secularism has partly provoked and partly spawned these substitute spiritualities. It has proved unattractive to many people, even though the assumptions that some secularists hold (such as a denial of any reality outside the dimensions of time and space) have influenced some new reconstructions of religious faith.

Despite the wishes of ardent secular atheists, religion may be undergoing many transformations in the contemporary world, but it is far from dying. The future of some mainstream religions, however, could seem under grave threat, at least in some parts of the globe. Are the days of Christianity numbered in large parts of Europe? Or can it transform itself into ways of faith that are relevant and challenging to twenty-first-century people?

A new religious reformation

Europe is certainly not quite the Christian continent it once was, even if that ideal has been romanticized by some of those who, like Pope Benedict XVI, appeal to a past they know only through a particular and idealized interpretation of it. Immigration and inter-continental movements by people for jobs and other opportunities provide challenges to, but also opportunities for, Christians to live and share faith.

There have been many population movements in the contemporary world. Some have been tragic, with refugees fleeing from genocide in large parts of Africa and elsewhere. At the beginning of 2006, the United Nations recognized over 20 million people uprooted because of war, famine, or some other mostly human-made tragedy.[15] Other emigrations have been voluntary. Large numbers of people have settled peacefully in other countries, in order to improve their quality of life. Countries in Europe and North America have sought immigrants to fill perceived needs in the employment market, and there has also been some illegal immigration. People have bought their religion with them.

Religions can be divisive in multicultural contexts. When two nations were carved out of British India in 1947, secular (but predominantly Hindu) India and Muslim Pakistan, up to one million people were killed in the migration of peoples across borders: Hindus from Pakistan to India; Muslims from India to Pakistan; Sikhs from Pakistan to India. Religious affiliation became the excuse for violence, torture and murder. When I lived for a while in a Pakistani village during the summer of 1985, where once there had been a small number of Hindus who emigrated to India at partition, some elderly residents told me that they could not understand the madness of those days, and why Hindu friends felt compelled to leave. They were too ashamed to admit straightforwardly their own complicity in what had happened, but their misery and contrition were palpable. And this 'madness' must have happened in many thousands of villages on both sides of the new borders. Religion has much to answer for, in how it was used in those circumstances by religious people. Hindus, Muslims and Sikhs had lived alongside each other for centuries, often peacefully, and with intermarriage, friendship and toleration. Actually, religious difference had not mattered at all until extraordinary circumstances (the division of their country by outsider, imperialist, departing British rulers) drove people into this collective insanity.

One response to intra-religious violence could be to wish for the end of religion, and to work to bring about that end. It was not, however, the response of the distinguished Canadian religionist Wilfred Cantwell Smith, who was a missionary in Lahore in the last days of undivided India. He was on leave during partition, and returned to a new country (Lahore having become part of Pakistan). He had just written a young man's book on *Modern Islam in India* (it was published in 1946); fine, in its way, but with a Marxist analysis that forced its subject, often unconvincingly, into that mould, and which underplayed the importance of religious commitment. Gazing on the ruins of Lahore, he felt them 'burnt into his consciousness'. He abandoned his Marxist analysis for a rather more profound and humane interpretation of faith, belief and the other component parts of religion. For the rest of his life, he taught and wrote about religion in ways that accepted its importance and helped men and women to understand it so that they would use it for good and not for ill. For Smith, then, the attempt to play down the importance of religion was monumental folly. The issue was how to understand and live it so as to harness its capacity for human flourishing rather than human destruction.[16]

It is not just in far-flung places that religion can divide and kill. The events of 11 September 2001 made US citizens and residents aware of the power of religion for evil, and those of 7 July 2005 impacted Britons directly. Indeed, the whole world was shocked by these attacks. Of course, US and British foreign policy had for some time exacerbated religious and other divisions in the Middle East and elsewhere, but (for example) the destruction of Lebanon in the 1970s and 1980s did not affect New Yorkers and Londoners with quite the same force as did the later events. The events of 9/11 and 7/7 have revealed just how alienated some young Muslims are in the West. Nothing can justify their horrors, but they are not best understood by a simplistic analysis that tells us how appalling all religion is, and Islam in particular. Many young Muslims who are attracted to terrorism were born and bred in the West and for a variety of reasons choose the path of Islamic 'fundamentalism'. Some but not all of these are to do with institutionalized racism, which means that many of their economic and other hopes go unfulfilled in British and US society.

Wilfred Cantwell Smith's moment of illumination among the ruins of Lahore, making him realize the need to encourage religious commitment to the common good so as to avoid such calamities, strikes a chord in many people of goodwill. Indeed, many excellent initiatives are happening in multifaith North America and Europe, though these often go unnoticed by people who are persuaded only by the stock clichés of a clash of civilizations and of religions as reactionary forces; clichés that many media sources purvey, uncritically. Many, many more Muslims make a significant, positive contribution to their country of immigration than turn from it in violence and disgust. For example, the Council on American–Islamic Relations does much to make people aware of the constructive involvement of American Muslims in US society.[17] Many local interfaith organizations in Britain (for example, in Glasgow, Wolverhampton, Leicester and Bradford) have brought not just Christians and Muslims together, but people of many faiths, and have resulted in their not just becoming friends but also working together to improve such things as local housing and education policies.[18] Neighbours in religiously diverse areas learn to like each other and to attend each others' weddings, eat each others' food, and share joys and sorrows together.

This interaction can be fruitful. Of course, there are mad mullahs, rabid rabbis, poisonous parsons, and other religious leaders who seek to divide communities from each other, either out of their paranoia pretending to represent truth, or because they have an understanding of God that is inadequate to the needs of divers societies and that falls short of being able to cope with his surprisingly inclusive love.[19] Still, ordinary people often act much better than the sermons they have heard encourage them to do.

One particularly notable current trend is that members of Diaspora religions (those that become rooted abroad in new places) can reform and restructure their faith in ways that make good sense of their new situation; better sense than some of the customs and convictions in their countries of origin. For example, it is delightful to talk with intelligent young Muslims in Glasgow or Chicago or Orange County, California, who are able to fashion new yet recognizably Islamic ways of understanding dress codes, roles for men and women, new forms of religious and secular education, and a host of other things, freed from the cultural assumptions that predominate in some parts of the world of Islam. They are excited about the possibility that this will cause a re-formation of Islam and speculate that this will eventually impact more traditional Muslim centres of learning and authority. Another example is the growing importance of western Buddhism, which has attracted many people in the USA and elsewhere. Some Buddhist leaders from traditionally Buddhist countries like Sri Lanka, Thailand and Tibet have suggested that the future of their religion lies as much in California as in Kathmandu. If so, Buddhism will look very different in the future than it does at present.

Christian faith has also gone through extraordinary transformations. One example is the new teaching in the Roman Catholic and some Protestant churches about Jews, which began with the reforms of the Second Vatican Council (1962–5) and, in particular, the seminal conciliar document *Nostra Aetate*.[20] Centuries of anti-Semitic teaching has been abandoned, and this has begun to impact and modify Christians' attitudes towards a wider range of religions and their understanding of God's mission in the world and their part in it. As important as the official teachings have been in renewing the Church, just as significant has been the renewal of the western churches by insights from theologians of the churches of Asia, Africa and elsewhere. Even more important, in the long term, may be the impact that immigration by Christians has on new countries. In Ireland, for example, mass attendance and priestly vocations have fallen dramatically in recent years yet, in some Irish communities, Polish and other immigration has re-energized the church. They bring their Irish partners back to church, and so breathe life back into an institution that has been eroded by the acids of modernity.[21]

A future for religion

There is no denying that modernity has proven to be a difficult epoch for religion. Ways of thinking and assumptions about how the world works have tended to marginalize traditional beliefs in God, and sometimes even claim to have utterly over-turned them.

Christianity seems increasingly beleaguered, irrelevant and out of touch in Europe. Empty churches across large swathes of the continent illustrate this. In large parts of the USA, it seems to have been captured by the dim, the greedy, the noisy and the self-righteous. Yet there are signs of hope, some of which we have indicated.

The decline in churchgoing has not heralded the end of religion, only its transformation into new forms. Occasionally, one is tempted to observe that the real alternative to religion has been not an austere, rationalist secularism, but bad religion mixed up with some of the less endearing characteristics of secularism, like greed and rampant individualism.

Is it possible to rescue religion from the wreckage? More specifically, has Christianity any hope of a future in Europe and other parts of the world where it struggles to speak words of salvation about a crucified God, whose nature and whose name is love?

This book contends that the answer to this question is: yes. But before we can understand how this can be so, we need to pay more attention to why we find ourselves in the state we are in. We turn to that issue in chapter 2.

2

Religion in the Christian West

Contemporary European Christianity can be painted in dark colours. To take only the United Kingdom as an example: a recent Tearfund report on churchgoing found that 4.9 million people attend a Christian place of worship weekly, about 10 per cent of the adult population; but that 32.2 million (two-thirds of UK adults) have no connection with church at all, or with any other religion.[1]

Down but not quite out

You do not really need a report to tell you what you can see for yourself. Many Christian acts of worship are performed in almost empty buildings, except for a few old people.

It could be claimed that mainstream churches are out of good leaders, as well as worshippers. A few years ago, a Methodist minister of some denominational distinction was talking gobbledegook and at length at a meeting of the World Council of Churches in Geneva. An official of that organization was taken aback when told of the man's eminence, paused for a moment, and then observed: 'Oh, well. Scum rises to the top.' Perhaps it is kinder to note that church leaders of considerable merit, like Archbishop Rowan Williams of Canterbury, are unable to make the distinguished contribution they could because of the mean-spirited obsession some of their national and international colleagues have with the wrong issues.

Indeed, it is difficult to see how effective and knowledgeable leadership can be offered in most mainstream churches, given the changes that have taken place in clergy education over the last 20 years or so. Many new clergy are taught part-time, and the reduced list of subjects to be learned often causes old-timers to shake their heads, ruefully. The days of all (or most) ordinands learning Greek (still less, Hebrew) so as to read the Bible carefully are long gone. The teaching of Systematic Theology often takes second place to Pastoral Theology which, while at its best a fairly useful ancillary discipline, often conspires with the therapeutic culture of our age to convince ordinands that how they and other people feel is more important than, for example, the truth about something. Some ordained people, or those seeking Christian leadership, certainly regard ministry in this curative way. My heart always sinks when trainee or actual pastors tell me that their favourite model for ministry is that of the wounded healer. Just occasionally, a wise minister knows what she is talking about, and attempts to do justice to the concept that Carl Jung proposed and Henri Nouwen elaborated. Many, however, interpret this model to mean that, because they themselves are hurt and injured people, they can sympathize or even empathize with kindred spirits and help to heal them. It does not work like that. Others do not exist so that we can get some sort of meaning for and resolution to our own conflicts by dealing with theirs. Rather (as Jung warned in rather more technical language than this) we are likely to harm them, and they us. Moreover, this therapeutic view of the Church suggests that it is full of people consumed with their own wants which, if true, is alarming. Jesus healed some people, to be sure; but he challenged and inspired them and many others. Not everybody who followed him was emotionally needy and spiritually immature.

I have heard theological college students pass over the chance to study church history on the grounds that it promotes patriarchy or some other evil; though how they know this in advance of any patient study of the evidence rarely troubles them; nor how they will recognize the triviality and glory of their own place in the sun if they do not know about other times and places. Even more bothersome is the capacity of some seminarians to play down the importance of what they are studying. Many want to have a qualification such as an MA (with a minimum of previous theological work as the price of admission), rather than to work out a vocation. Some second-career seminary students assume that their previous experience is of immeasurable value to pastoral ministry. Sometimes it is, yet mostly it is not. Being a preacher, a prophet and a pastor is a hard calling, and it is not immediately obvious that a previous career as a teacher or a bank official or a social worker or a homemaker will have nurtured it (or pre-qualified them to 'have gained those skills', as one pompous person put it to me, rather illustrating why I thought he could never be the man for ministry that he thought he already was). I used to observe to my students that anyone from these worthy professions (and many more) who went to medical school for his second career, convinced he was ready to perform heart surgery, might find a cool response if he were to argue his case to the school's dean.

Some Christian congregations are growing, and fast, particularly in the evangelical tradition. But often their view of God (in other words, their theology) seems to outsiders to be trivial, far removed from the teachings of Jesus of Nazareth. Many Methodists who sing 'Majesty, worship his majesty; unto Jesus be glory, honour and praise' seem to have forgotten Charles Wesley's magnificent interpretation of Paul's insight about the incarnation of Jesus, that:

Emptied of his majesty,
Of his dazzling glories shorn,
Being's source begins to be,
And God himself is born![2]

37

Many evangelical choruses have a Christology (convictions about Jesus) that does not measure up to the standards of orthodox Trinitarian theology. A Muslim who listens in would think that Islam's conviction that Christians worship a man, instead of God, have been proven correct.

Our subject here is Christianity in Europe, and the UK in particular. But it is worth a passing glance across the Atlantic Ocean. I sometimes tell my students, only half-jokingly, that there is too little religion in Europe and too much in the USA, where regular churchgoing is much more the norm. Actually, a number of different statistics (mostly out of date and far from convincing in some of their figures and how they are reached) suggest that about 40 per cent of US residents attend church regularly;[3] a large number, but still less than those who do not. People often have the impression that many churchgoers, especially in the South, are merely members of the right wing of the Republican Party at prayer. Or else they are easily duped: US television has a number of channels dedicated to 'Christian leaders', often self-appointed, who seem to find it easy to get gullible people to write cheques to them, by promising them everything from a prosperous lifestyle to a cure for some vile disease or physical impairment. Christian faith may be doing better in the USA than in Europe, but its shriller spokespeople often advocate positions that are hard to equate with the teachings of Jesus.

In reality, despite this gloomy picture, there are signs of hope. Many ordained people are wise, integrated and godly. Moreover, the Church cannot just be judged by the quality of its clergy and other leaders, though a spiritually healthy church is likely to have ministers who have had the opportunity to test their vocation, prayerfully, in an atmosphere of learning, and for a reasonable period of time. Some evangelical congregations have discovered a social dimension to their religion, and their pastors are not just interested in personal salvation or other less desirable forms of individual advantage. Lots of people in the pews are well adjusted, and are not there because they are sad, mad or bad. Some have seen beyond the individualistic and therapeutic spirit of the age, and wish to be part of the Christian vocation to point to the signs of God's kingly rule and to live out its demands.

Students of church history are aware that the Church has been in difficult positions before. This is not the only age with untrained and self-obsessed clergy, the wrong priorities and empty churches, or with some other defects. Christianity has, in other times and places, been trivial, prone to violence, self-centred, in thrall to the spirit of the age rather than God's Spirit. Yet it has muddled through, reformed itself, and been a vehicle of salvation and hope for many.

Still, it will not do to hope against hope that something will turn up and get Christianity out of its present state in Europe. It is, observably, in a fine mess, even if there are some grounds for optimism. Something needs to be done about it. Christian teaching tells us that we are co-partners with God in his creation, ruling it on his behalf and as he would wish (Genesis 1.26–31). But before we ask what we can do with God to help fix the Church and mend the world, we need to ask how the present situation has come about. Although Christian faith has been in difficult situations before, there are a series of overlapping reasons that have contributed to its present situation in Europe (and in other places where English-speaking Europeans have settled) and that we need to understand if we are to do something constructive about it.

Christianity and violence

> Put your sword back into its place; for all who take the sword
> will perish by the sword. (Matthew 26.52)

So Jesus, when he was seized in the Garden of Gethsemane, addresses a follower who struck out at a slave of the high priest, severing his ear. Christians in the earliest days of the faith had no power, and most had no desire to take on imperial Rome by show of force. Paul and other Christian leaders shared the conviction of many of their contemporaries that civil war, which had engulfed the Roman Empire for much of the first century BCE until the reign of Augustus (d. 14 CE), was a terrible thing. Hence Paul could write: 'Let every person be subject to the governing authorities; for there is no authority except from God, and those authorities that exist have been instituted by God' (Romans 13.1). That verse has been used by later Christians to justify state oppression, but such was not Paul's intention. He knew that government officials could abuse their power and kill innocent people, including Jesus, but he also knew of the appalling consequences of anarchy. In fact, if Roman peace had not permitted the building and maintenance of roads and other forms of communication, so that people could travel peacefully over considerable distances, it is unlikely that Paul and others could have founded churches in the Mediterranean world of the day.

In the first few centuries, Christian faith did not spread by violent persecution of others, and its spread throughout the Roman Empire was gradual. Maybe about 10 per cent of the empire was Christian before the Emperor Constantine I granted Christianity favourable treatment at the beginning of the fourth century. Christianity's rapid rise to pre-eminence was confirmed in 381, when it became the official religion of the empire under Theodosius I.

The distinguished Christian scholar of Islam, Kenneth Cragg, has offered a thoughtful distinction between Jesus and Muhammad, as they contemplated the success of their prophetic vocations. Jesus in Gethsemane eschewed violence, even at the cost of apparent failure; whereas Muhammad was prepared to defend God and his developing community of faith, by force if necessary. Cragg is a distinguished scholar, not a tawdry controversialist, and was trying to identify a genuine difference between the two religious leaders, not to score cheap points. He has a point about the origins of the Christian and Islamic faiths. However, things are not so simple in terms of their developing histories. To be sure, Christian faith spread peacefully during its early centuries, whereas the early spread of Islam was part of a great military success story. But Christians have not always followed the peaceful teachings of Jesus.

There is verbal violence in the writings of the early fathers of the Church. Some of this is not as bad as it seems to us now, but followed the written, and especially the spoken, rhetorical conventions of the day, which were more forthright and even abusive than is considered appropriate in many circles today. However, as Christians acquired political and other forms of power in the later Roman Empire, physical violence began to infect Christians' discourse with each other. To take just one example, on Christmas Eve 361 an angry mob in Alexandria killed their patriarch, and paraded his corpse around the city. Bishop George was a foreigner from Cappadocia in modern Turkey, with different views from most Egyptians of his day about the relationship of Jesus to God. That was an age when market traders in the great cities of the Eastern Empire, such as Constantinople and Alexandria, would argue over such an issue. Nowadays, some European Christians might envy the importance of religion to the man and woman in the street then, stirring in them passion and commitment, not always knowing that religion is still like that in some parts of the world. But it came at a price, on those occasions when differences of belief turned to fisticuffs, mob fury, violence and murder.

The medieval European world that eventually succeeded the collapse of the Western Roman Empire was one of much violence, in which Christian beliefs were implicated. The crusades, which occurred at intervals throughout the High Middle Ages, caused not only the deaths of Jews and Muslims in the Holy Land, but also anti-Semitic riots in German and other cities, leading to the deaths of European Jews. In calling for the liberation of the Holy Land from Muslim rule at the council of Clermont in 1095, Pope Urban II singled Jews out for special mention. He laid down the principle that 'if it be a good deed to kill and mistreat Mussulmans, it could not be a sin to massacre unbelieving Jews'. As a result of public statements like these, there were massacres of Jews at Speyer, Worms and Mainz. Maybe 5,000 Jews died.

What of the chief aim of the crusaders, to liberate Jerusalem from the rule of the ungodly? The crusaders took Jerusalem by force in July 1099. Muslims were slain indiscriminately. When the chronicler of that first crusade, Raymond of Aguilers, went to visit the Temple area on the morning of 15 July, he picked his way through corpses and blood that reached to his knees. The Jews of Jerusalem fled to their chief synagogue. They were held to have aided and abetted Muslims, so the crusaders burned the synagogue to the ground and the Jews were incinerated in it. This went some way towards achieving the ambition of a leader of the first crusade, Godfrey of Bouillon, who had sworn to avenge the blood of Christ and 'leave no single member of the Jewish race alive'.[4]

A later crusading army, on the way to the Holy Land, where few of them ever arrived, took a diversion and sacked Constantinople, seat of Eastern Christianity and of Byzantium. So, in 1204, western Christians were killing eastern Christians instead of Jews and Muslims. Pope Innocent III, who had approved a crusade to the Holy Land but not against other Christians, was outraged:

How, indeed, is the Greek church to be brought back into ecclesiastical union and to a devotion for the Apostolic See when she has been beset with so many afflictions and persecutions that she sees in the Latins only an example of perdition and the works of darkness, so that she now, and with reason, detests the Latins more than dogs? As for those who were supposed to be seeking the ends of Jesus Christ, not their own ends, whose swords, which they were supposed to use against the pagans, are now dripping with Christian blood, they have spared neither age nor sex.[5]

Schism between the Eastern and Western Churches had come to a head in 1054, ostensibly over a relatively abstruse issue of theology (did the Spirit proceed from the Father and the Son, as the Western Church maintained; or only from the Father, as the Eastern Church held?), though with many other factors involved. Pope Innocent wrote less than a century later when there was still hope of some reconciliation. The event of 1204 was part of a long weakening of Byzantium's power, which came to an end in 1453 with the capture of Constantinople by Ottoman Muslim Turks. Eastern Christians still blame the Western Church for undermining their political power and leaving them open to foreign conquest. Unsurprisingly, relations between the Roman Catholic Church and the Orthodox Patriarchate of Constantinople (now Istanbul) are still tense, despite recent endeavours of Popes John Paul II and Benedict XVI to improve them.

When the Western Church split at the Reformation into the Roman Catholic and many Protestant churches, violence in the name of religion still plagued Europe, directed as before, both towards non-Christians and against Christians of other persuasions. It is possible and desirable to give only a few examples. The Inquisition plagued Europe and later the Americas from the end of the twelfth century onwards, and was not formally abolished until 1834. The French Wars of Religion included the notorious St Bartholomew's Day massacre of Huguenots (Protestants), starting in Paris on 24 August 1572, and spreading to other places in France. The Thirty Years War ravaged central Europe from 1618 to 1648, killing perhaps about 20 per cent of Germans through armed conflict, disease and famine, and was in part a religious conflict between Catholics, Lutherans and Calvinists. The execution of King Charles I at the end of the English Civil Wars in January 1649 had religious roots. The Glorious Revolution of 1688 removed the Catholic King James II, replacing him with his Protestant daughter, Mary II, and her husband William III. John and Charles Wesley lived through two Jacobean rebellions of 1715 and 1745, aimed at restoring the Catholic Stuart dynasty to the thrones of England and Scotland. One could go on, wearisomely. The point is surely made that religious differences continued to tear Europe apart in the early modern period.

In his sermon (92) on zeal, John Wesley observed that, although without zeal we cannot progress in religion, the irony is that 'nothing has done more disservice to religion, or more mischief to mankind, than a sort of zeal which has for several ages prevailed, both in Pagan, Mahometan, and Christian nations. Insomuch that it may truly be said, pride, covetousness, ambition, revenge, have in all parts of the world slain their thousands; but zeal its ten thousands.'[6]

By the time Wesley preached his sermon, many people were wearied by the misguided zeal of much religion, which led many of its followers to do violence against other believers. Not just the eastern Mediterranean but much of Europe had been drenched in bloodshed, in the name of religion. Enough was enough.

And is it true?

If a long and wearisome history of its involvement in violence was one strand in the decline of religion in Europe, another was a rising scepticism about religious truth claims among some intellectuals.

Such scepticism was not new, but there was more of it about in post-Reformation Europe. Plato records that, in the fifth century BCE, Protagoras observed that 'man is the measure of all things'. He was banished from Athens and his books were burned in the marketplace for repudiating the city's gods. He observed: 'About the gods, I do not have [the capacity] to know, whether they are or are not, nor to know what they are like in form; for there are many things that prevent this knowledge: the obscurity [of the issue] and the shortness of human life.'

Incidences of atheism can be found in many cultures, and come in a number of forms. It can be the practical atheism of those who may theoretically affirm (or at least not deny) a transcendent element to life, but live as if there were not. So the Old Testament psalmist twice affirmed that 'Fools say in their heart, "There is no God"' (Psalms 14.1 and 53.1). Or it can be a philosophical conviction that there is insufficient data to make a judgement about the existence of God. The twentieth-century English philosopher Bertrand Russell was asked what he would say if, after death, God asked him why he had not been a believer. He replied, 'Not enough evidence, God! Not enough evidence.' (It is arguable that Russell was looking for the wrong kind of evidence and in the wrong places.) A more telling philosophical critique of religion is that which undermines some of the arguments that some believers use to point to the truth of religion, but which are not necessarily very compelling. The first-century BCE Roman philosopher and poet Lucretius was a sceptic, observing, in his poem *De Rerum Natura* (About the Nature of Things), that 'to such heights of evil are people driven by religion'. He argued that for people to contemplate eternal extinction is no worse than pondering the nothingness from which they came, a rather neat riposte to those people for whom belief in God is mostly to do with making sense, not of the mystery and wonder of life, but of the fear of death. One could include criticisms of many of the classical arguments for the existence of God: the ontological argument; the argument from design; the cosmological argument; and others.

Lucretius' argument is somewhat close to the position of the seventeenth-century English philosopher, John Locke. By the early modern period, Renaissance humanism had persuaded a number of people of the truth of Protagoras' observation, and so, gradually, more and more philosophers and other thinkers looked to human endeavour rather than divine guidance in order to frame laws for the common good. Locke, for example, thought that human nature was reasonable and tolerant, and that the mind is a *tabula rasa* (blank slate) on which experiences leave their mark: people are not born with innate ideas that are knowable without experience. He also believed that the knowledge of God could be deduced from intuition and reasoning alone. Here was a ticking time bomb directed at Christian views that God must reveal himself through Scripture if humans are to know of him and his ways.

Locke was not the first major modern philosopher to undermine traditional Christian views of God. An earlier candidate for that prize was the Frenchman René Descartes, who died in 1560. He had the ambitious project to rebuild philosophy from new and, in his unfinished *Rules for the Direction of the Understanding*, he stated an equally ambitious principle that, just as certainty is the goal of mathematics, so it must be for philosophy. He tried to ascertain how to make different sorts of belief free from doubt. The only one to emerge from this test was belief in his own existence. He then appealed to God as that which is objective and independent from himself, in order to validate his argument. But this is hardly a traditional argument for the necessity of God, and his own defence of God consisted in variations on the cosmological and ontological arguments; unconvincing and half-hearted explanations, as if he vaguely realized that placing God in these gaps in his argument would not do.

It is unsurprising that later European and some North American philosophers began to lose the knack of including God as a crucial element in their reflections. The eighteenth-century Scot, David Hume, was regarded by some of his contemporaries as an unbeliever (though he himself claimed never to have met an atheist), and denied university preferment on that account. He believed that the Christian religion was born in a complex of miracles, which one is bound to believe if one is a Christian. He defined miracles as violations of the laws of nature, and as such unlikely to occur. The publication of his *Dialogues Concerning Natural Religion* was delayed until after his death, possibly to avoid further conflict with the Church and many conventional believers. His posthumously published book describes the origins and development of religious beliefs; their origins are seen as non-rational, or even irrational. Early humans were polytheistic and invoked some 'invisible intelligence' to understand uncontrollable natural occurrences, like sickness and earthquakes. Monotheism replaced the worship of many gods; it is hardly an advance, because of its dogmatism and intolerance, and because its appeal to reason corrupted philosophical thought and created ridiculous and bigoted theological systems. However, religion is not universal in the way that our non-rational beliefs in causation or physical objects are. Indeed, Hume believed that some nations reject religion or simply do not have it. Therefore, there is hope that humans will eventually outgrow religion. The *Dialogues Concerning Natural Religion* is a remarkable book, anticipating Victorian notions of religious evolution by a century, and asking hard questions of believers that undergraduates and others still do well to ponder. Still, many of Hume's views about religion and early peoples are based more on guesswork or even wishful thinking than on any empirical evidence.

Hume, who regarded many prevalent religious beliefs as 'sick men's dreams' and who thought of the world as 'an inexplicable mystery', probably helped to hasten the end of the influence of Deism in Britain, which had a far more rosy view of God and the world. Deism flourished in Britain from the last years of the seventeenth century until the middle years of the eighteenth. It was also popular in France, and in the USA, where it influenced some of the founding fathers as they put together the constitution in 1787. A diverse and multi-faceted phenomenon, it rejected divine revelation, and so was suspicious of holy books, clergy, and the teachings and institutions of Christianity and other religions. It promoted reason and morality. Many Deists believed that God created the world but mostly did not interfere in its day-to-day running, though after death he would reward people for their good deeds. In their mind, God was rather like an upper-class English gentleman, for whom excessive work and any undue interference in the doings of others would be unseemly and vulgar. Deists respected Jesus as a moral exemplar, but denied the doctrinal claims made for him by the Church. Some regarded themselves as Christians but, for many of their 'spiritual' and academic heirs, Deism proved to be a bridge to modern agnosticism and atheism.

The Deists' attitude towards divine revelation meant that they did not venerate the Bible, even though they doffed their caps towards the universe's absentee landlord, God. This would have appalled the sixteenth-century Protestant reformers who, in bringing the Bible closer to the people by encouraging translations into the vernacular, had intended to make God and his word living and active in the lives of ordinary people. While that was the result for many people, over time some men and women began to notice apparent mistakes, inconsistencies, muddled arguments, and all sorts of related faults that most books, to some extent, contain. It became possible, even to some extent natural, to treat the Bible as a human production. You might respect its contents more than most works, since it deals with the high theme of God, but it was not necessary to ascribe sole authorship or even overall editorial responsibility to God. Indeed, if you were a believer and a careful reader of the Bible, you had either to ignore obvious problems in scriptural consistency, or manufacture reasons why they were not the problems they seemed to be, or else rescue God from the fallibilities of Scripture by recognizing a human element in its production. Nowadays, the Bible is widely bought and widely unread. Some contemporary readers, like Christopher Hitchens, adopt an attitude of disdain towards it: Hitchens refers to 'The Nightmare of the "Old" Testament'; and he claims that 'The New Testament Exceeds the Evil of the "Old" One'. Intriguingly, he interprets Scripture much as the Christian fundamentalists do with whom he has such issues; careful thought and reflection are no more within his exegetical grasp than within theirs. We have moved a considerable distance from reverence to derision, and from careful attention to detail to the trivial assertion of prejudices, in the last 500 years of reading Scripture.

Baruch Spinoza, a seventeenth-century Dutch Jew of Portuguese ancestry, was an early critic of Scripture; critic, in that he applied critical standards to it; he was not a prototype of the Hitchens school of generalized contempt, though his religious views brought down the condemnation of many believers upon his head. In July 1656, the Sephardic Jewish community of Amsterdam issued a writ of *cherem*, similar to excommunication, against him, which was never withdrawn. Among other unconventional beliefs, he denied the providential action of God in history, and the status of Jews as the chosen people. He rejected the core Jewish conviction that God gave the Mosaic Law to Jews and that it was binding upon them. He noticed that there are problems with the traditional Jewish and Christian view of the Mosaic authorship of the Pentateuch: the references to Moses in the third person; the account of his death and of events after that; and the fact that some of the places are called by names that postdated Moses. Spinoza thought that a single person, probably Ezra, was the editor of these and some other biblical writings, collating them centuries later in the post-exilic period. He regarded the prophetic writings as 'heaped together' many years after the facts they record. Spinoza was not the first person to notice problems with traditional views of biblical authorship, though he was a very distinguished and early example. More important, he drew the conclusion that you must examine the Bible as you would any other historical document: you look at the data of Scripture itself, and evaluate it rationally. His (somewhat questionable) judgement was that, in this way, Scripture would prove to be an ethical rather than a philosophical or doctrinal artefact, encouraging its readers to love God and their neighbour.

From the eighteenth century onwards, biblical criticism became a growing and eventually a reputable intellectual pursuit. The German H. S. Reimarus, who died in 1768, was a Deist who believed that a natural religion, worked out by reason, was the right way to go: one that acknowledged the existence of a wise and beneficent creator, and the immortality of the soul. Relying upon Scripture for knowledge of God is a dead end: the Bible is full of errors; it contradicts experience, rationality and ethics, and has no proper belief in immortality. Writers of the New Testament served their own ambitions, and were frauds, as was Jesus. The Bible is no proper revelation and, even if it were, revelation cannot compare with reason as the basis for a truly moral and spiritual life.

Biblical criticism came to concentrate on a number of areas: authorship, meaning, and other disciplines. From early on, its findings affected and even undermined traditional Christian understandings of Jesus. Many early critics were predisposed to assume that treating the Bible as a human document would deny Jesus any divine status. Even so, they were not ready simply to dismiss his importance out of hand. Some of them were, indeed, evidently attracted to aspects of the personality they believed they could detect through the encrustations of the evangelists' misplaced piety. David Friedrich Strauss's *Life of Jesus* appeared to great acclaim in Germany in 1835, and was translated into English by no less a figure than the novelist George Eliot. But the most engaging nineteenth-century life of Jesus was by the Frenchman Ernest Renan. He studied for the Catholic priesthood but quit before ordination, due mainly to his critical reading of the Bible. He spent time in the Middle East and published his *La Vie de Jésus* in 1863. It was greeted by a storm of controversy. It is a book still worth reading, not least to see through the criticisms of the devout and the adulation of the sceptics, to the charming if over-romantic work beyond them. In it Jesus is a wonderful man; not God, no, but a man like none other. For Renan, the Sermon on the Mount will never be surpassed, and its author breathed and even created 'the pure spirit of religion'. Unlike, say, the second-century Roman Emperor Marcus Aurelius and some other ethical teachers, Jesus 'remains an inexhaustible principle of moral regeneration for humanity'. So it is that 'among the sons of men there is none born who is greater than Jesus'. Even so, he did no miracles, for miracles can never happen, and he was not God's son in any mainstream Christian understanding of what that means. The disciples did not exactly make up the resurrection, but their ardent expectations and excited nerves, and Mary Magdalene's hallucinatory experience, misled them into a false understanding of their master and of what happened at the end of his life. Renan's work has had an influence up to this day, not least in some areas of Jewish–Christian dialogue, where it is felt that interpreting Jesus as an (or even, the) exemplary moral teacher of Israel could prove a bridge between the two religions. As early as 1924, Joseph Klausner, a Lithuanian Jew, portrayed Jesus in such a way, at a time when many Jews thought of him, if at all, in a negative light, because of the long history of Christian anti-Semitism. Echoes of this approach are found in the more recent writings of Geza Vermes, by origins a Hungarian Jew, who became a Roman Catholic priest and then reverted to his Jewish roots.[7]

However, for all its charm and influence, Renan's is an extraordinarily sentimental work; reading it is like wading through treacle. And, although he attributes high ethical standards to Jesus, his Jesus was not above shoddy manipulation, such as pretending to raise Lazarus from the dead; it was a fraud worked with some of his disciples, aimed at impressing the masses. *La Vie de Jésus* has also provided the basis for polemical attacks upon Jesus and Christian faith, by those who read such stuff rather more carefully than they scrutinize the original documents of early Christianity. For example, the Indian Muslim judge and controversialist, Syed Ameer Ali, in his life of the Prophet Muhammad published in 1873, drew material from *La Vie de Jésus* in order to portray the founder of Christianity as ineffectual and somewhat effete, and surrounded by followers who were not worthy of him. By contrast, Muhammad proclaimed a vital religion and had brave and trustworthy colleagues. (Ameer Ali's work was called *A Critical Examination of the Life and Teachings of Mohammed*, the first biography of the Prophet ever written in English by a Muslim, and was produced while he was a student in London, reading for the bar.)

By the nineteenth century, a small but significant number of middle-class and upper-class British intellectuals was sceptical of religious claims to truth.

Many more working-class Britons had also become alienated from religion. The chief cause of this was the effect of the Industrial Revolution, which began in England in the middle of the eighteenth century and eventually spread throughout much of the world. As a result of technological and other changes that transformed the working lives of many of its inhabitants, England became more urban than rural. The dislocation of people's lives as they moved from the countryside to towns or cities, where they mostly lived in poverty and squalor with little time for anything other than working and sleeping, broke any ties they had to local churches or hallowed communal religious obligations. Nineteenth-century novelists like Charles Dickens recorded the bleak conditions in which the working classes lived, and the resulting crime, hardening of hearts, and general misery. Dickens knew about childhood despair for, although he came from a relatively prosperous family, his father spent time in a debtors' prison, having spent too much money trying to keep up social appearances. At 12 years old, Charles worked a ten-hour day in a shoe-polish factory, to help support his family. In many cases, the established Church was not quick enough to respond to social changes, as is well illustrated in the novels of Anthony Trollope, George Eliot and other writers.

On the contrary, the working classes in the USA never lost their sense of identity with religion in the way that their peers in Britain did. The USA is a mostly immigrant nation, where many settled after fleeing from religious persecution in their land of origin. That folk memory underlines much of the rhetoric in US public life about 'the land of freedom' (often absurdly framed as though it were the only 'free' country in the world) and 'the separation of church and state' (which often, to the outsider, seems quite untrue; at the very least, the dividing wall leaks). Religion, particularly Protestant Christian religion, is part of the national genetic coding in the USA. Maybe this will change: only recently, Protestant Christians ceased to form more than half the population of the USA; and many mainstream Christian denominations, though they enjoy a level of commitment that is the envy of similar British churches, struggle more than once they did to fill their pews.

That struggle is not as serious as it is in Britain, where church-going has been a declining habit for a longer time. The English poet and inspector of schools Matthew Arnold probably wrote 'Dover Beach' during his honeymoon in 1851, though it was published later, in 1867. No doubt his agnostic attitude towards religion greatly irritated his father, as much as his eccentric use of his honeymoon must have perturbed his wife. Thomas had died in 1842 and was an advocate of a relatively liberal and very muscular Christianity; he was the author of *Tom Brown's Schooldays*. His son's 'Dover Beach' captures a certain Victorian mood of religious scepticism, assuming the imminent end of faith:

The Sea of Faith
Was once, too, at the full, and round earth's shore

Lay like the folds of a bright girdle furled.
But now I only hear
Its melancholy, long, withdrawing roar,
Retreating, to the breath
Of the night-wind, down the vast edges drear
And naked shingles of the world.

A new understanding of religion

These strands of scepticism about God, and faith, and Jesus and
other related religious, mostly Christian, issues, have been
played out against a changing understanding of the concept of
religion itself. Modern Europeans have interpreted 'religion'
differently from their forebears, without always knowing that
they have done so. There have been many recent attempts to
examine what precisely these differences are and how they
arose, though much of this debate has been less a case of intellectual sticks being rubbed together to produce warmth and
light, and more a loud sound of axes grinding.

It is in fact extraordinarily difficult to understand other times
and places. The opening of L. P. Hartley's 1953 novel *The Go-
between* asserts that 'The past is a foreign country: they do
things differently there.' Many scholars over the last 150 years
or so who have paid attention to the role of religion in society
are nonchalantly confident about their theories of religion,
partly because they have not paid heed to Hartley's arresting
point. They have often formulated their views and systems as if
ideas can exist with some kind of universal meaning or meanings that any sensible person can agree upon, independently of
the people who hold them and the circumstances in which they
live. And, as we shall see, many have assumed that they live in
advanced societies, far developed from more primitive times,
and have been blithely unaware of their racism and other un-
endearing false, secular dogmas. So we need to proceed with

caution if we are to locate changes in the modern and post-modern world's interpretation of religion.

The word 'religion' derives from the Latin word *religio* and so has European, specifically Roman, origins. It had a variety of interrelated meanings. Probably it originally meant reverence for the gods, then later referred to the rites offered to them. Most likely it came from *religare*, 'to bind things together', which emphasizes religion's communal obligations. To adapt an idea from John Wesley, there is no such thing as an individual religious person. Religions have almost always had things to say about such things as who you can marry, what you can eat and wear, and the duties that are required towards your own and wider groups of people. The modern western privatization of religion would look selfish and scandalous to most cultures in other times or places. It is just possible that not *religare* but another Latin word, *relegere*, is at the root of 'religion', which would give it a sense of 'to pass over things repeatedly'. If so (and maybe one does not have to choose between them), then this stresses religion's commitment to, even obsession with, custom and precedent. Once again, this flies in the face of contemporary tendencies to ignore the wisdom of the past and to forge spirituality on the anvil of personal preference and need.

If we are to trace a line from these original meanings of religion to how it has come to be interpreted in Europe's present and recent past, then we can hardly do better than to begin with a comment by the Canadian scholar, Wilfred Cantwell Smith. We have already met him standing before the ruins of Lahore after the partition of India and seeing in that experience the ruins of his own unconvincing attempts to depict South Asian Islam from a thoroughgoing Marxist perspective. For Smith, who died in 2000, religion was about humans. As a historian, he was sceptical of theories that confuse interesting ideas, even the idea of religion itself, with the religious faith and practice of most humans. In his ground-breaking book, *The Meaning and End of Religion*, first published in 1962, he wrote that the modern western world has made a mistake in 'mentally making religion into a thing, gradually coming to conceive it as an objective systematic entity'.[8] In fact, Smith believed that, for most people, religion consists of human faith and the cumulative tradition of rites and actions and beliefs and other such things from which they draw sustenance for their faith. So the medieval western world consisted mostly of people who lived their lives out of Christian understandings of faith and belief. Religion was part of the fabric of medieval European society; just as it is of many non-European countries to this day, and almost always has been. Until recently (this is changing to some extent with the effects of globalization), few people outside Europe and places populated by people of European origin would have thought it possible to conceive of a society without religious obligations, or to locate within it a specific and separate thing called 'religion'.

One result of the European Renaissance and the Protestant Reformation was to change the place of religion from being part of the texture of society to being identified as a discrete, separate, component part of it. A significant stage in that process was marked by the terms of the Peace of Westphalia, which brought to an end the Thirty Years War in central Europe in 1648. It re-established the principle of *cuius regio, eius religio* ('whose region, his religion'), a phrase that was probably coined in 1612 by the jurist Joachim Stephani to describe the outcome of the Peace of Augsburg in 1555, which divided Germany into Catholic and Protestant regions, determined by the faith of their ruler. The Peace of Westphalia affirmed the Peace of Augsburg, and added Calvinism as a third religious choice. Each prince had the right to select and enforce the religion in his territories.

Stephani's use of *religio* was very unusual. In medieval Europe, *religio* was mostly used to denote the state of life of a member of a religious order. Only after the collapse of the medieval world did it become customary to use 'religion' in the modern sense, so as to distinguish Catholics from Protestants and Calvinists. Religion was becoming a choice: in 1648, as in 1555, the decision of a prince; but by, say, 1848 or 1948 it could easily become a personal choice; and the choice might include the possibility of opting out of religion altogether.

This detachment of religion from the warp and woof of society, and its subsequent 'objectification', meant that Renaissance and especially Enlightenment thinkers began to assume that it could and should be explored through scientific enquiry, like any other natural object.

By the Victorian era in Britain (1837–1901), religion had become a 'thing', ripe for studying with tools provided by advances in science and what came to be known as the social sciences.

A search for the origins of religion

Once people began to think of religion as an object, it was only a matter of time before they began to ask the obvious question: what is this 'thing' called religion for?

If religion is about a super-person called God, who created the world in seven days and who will bring it to an end after the return of Jesus, then Darwinian and other forms of scientific enquiry could be judged to have dealt it a mortal blow in the middle years of the nineteenth century. And it was, indeed, the case that many educated people began to doubt the truth of Christian religion in the years that followed the publication of Darwin's findings in 1859 as *On the Origin of Species by Means of Natural Selection, or the Preservation of Favoured Races in the Struggle for Life.*

Plenty of people know the story of the supposedly arrogant Bishop Samuel Wilberforce (son of William, the famously successful advocate of the abolition of slavery) who debated with Thomas Huxley at the Oxford Union on 30 June 1860, about

Darwin's theory of evolution. At one point, Wilberforce asked Huxley whether it was through his grandfather or grandmother that he was descended from a monkey. Huxley's reply was to the effect that, given the choice between having an ape as a grandfather, or a talented man who introduced ridicule into an important discussion, he would plump for the former. It would seem like game, set and match to the enlightened and dignified freethinker over the absurd, boorish and reactionary churchman. Yet, truth to tell, this repartee never happened; it was a journalistic invention of the 1890s. Wilberforce had written a review about the subject beforehand, which no doubt formed the basis of his speech, and which Darwin himself had read and regarded as 'uncommonly clever'. It is worth recording the spurious elaboration of this incident as an illustration of the irreconcilable division into which science and religion were partitioned by some of their contenders, abetted by the press. So it could seem that rational, cool-headed, wise scientists must inevitably clash in a kind of ongoing dualistic duel with irrational religious bigots until the truth wins out. As it happens, like many Europeans of his day Huxley was a racist, using science to 'prove' that the black man will not 'be able to compete successfully with his bigger-brained and smaller-jawed rival [the white man], in a contest which is to be carried on by thoughts and not by bites'.

This persisting separation between religion and science, which could and should have been avoided, has led some scientists of our own day, like Richard Dawkins, Sam Harris and Victor Stenger, to take up arms against religion as the source of darkness, with as much misplaced and muddle-headed fervour as some Christians have shown towards Darwinian and other scientific notions.

Darwin's account of the origin of species through natural selection was an epochal moment in the human understanding of how scientific method can contribute to the knowledge of how the world is as it is and, in particular, how humans and other natural phenomena came to be. It could seem, at a stroke, to take away the need for religion, if religion is a 'thing' to which one turns instead for the same sort of information as scientists do, foolishly or simply out of ignorance. Developing understandings in physics and the other hard sciences have also relieved religion of the responsibility of deciding such things as, for example, the age of the world. In 1644, while the English Civil War was raging, Bishop John Lightfoot, Vice-Chancellor of Cambridge University, worked out that the world was created on Sunday, 12 September, 3928 BCE. In 1650, the Irish Archbishop, James Ussher, published his calculations that the world was created on Sunday, 23 October, 4004 BCE, beginning at sunset on the 22nd. Three centuries later, science can propose a better range of answers, and make these competing divines seem naïve, irrelevant and foolish.

So, if religion is *not* for understanding questions about human origins and the universe, because scientific methodology can do that so much better, what is it for? By the time of Darwin, many sceptics were coming to believe that religion was simply redundant; it was an outdated attempt by which primitive or unenlightened people answered issues that have now been proved to be better handled elsewhere. Such issues included 'Who made the world?', 'What is the importance of humans?' and similar questions which religion, if responsible for, handled in unscientific or pre-scientific and therefore false ways.

This developing religious scepticism was aided and abetted by the fact that Darwin's theories provided mid- and late-Victorians with a mostly unquestioned intellectual assumption that, just as species have developed over time through a process of natural selection, so this can be extended to the realm of human society. The term 'social Darwinism' first appeared in an article published in 1879. Many middle and later nineteenth-century writers assumed that humans had progressed to the advanced state of humans in their own time and place. Two world wars and many genocides have still not quite destroyed this heady idea.

With the rise of the social sciences in the nineteenth century, sociologists, anthropologists, psychologists, political and other 'soft' scientists began to articulate what their emerging disciplines could reveal about this human 'progress'. Since human awe in the face of the mysteries of life and death is one of the earliest known characteristics of our species, perhaps indeed the earliest, and because this wonder was known to reveal itself in rites and 'holy' artefacts and institutions, it was necessary for these nascent social scientists to provide a theory or theories of religion as part of their interpretation of human progress.

If religion is not founded in a revelatory sense of God, then we have to account for it some other way or ways. And so there grew up a search for the 'real' origins of religion. Different thinkers and disciplines saw it as a means of affirming social identity, or as offering consolation for the sufferings that arise from political powerlessness, or as a product of the human mind struggling with meanings that it cannot always acknowledge. And so on. Some of these great scholars, though they for the most part did not believe that God or the gods were ontological realities, were not exactly unsympathetic to religion, and saw it as having a useful, even critical, function in the course of humanity's history. For example, one of the founders of sociology, Emile Durkheim, by birth a Jew, then a Catholic, but an atheist for most of his life, saw the gods as useful social constructs created to explain the way individuals behave in society. Others, however, like Karl Marx and Sigmund Freud, were far less friendly to religion, and readers can sense the hostility in their writings.

Nowadays, scholars from the social sciences and religious studies have an interesting relationship. Some assume that the academic study of religion is naturally located within the social sciences. Religion is, in this view, not really a clearly defined discipline but rather a field of study, and each of the social sciences can contribute, in some measure, towards understanding how religion originated in a way or ways that their discipline best explains. Those scholars of religion who have no personal faith themselves, and who cannot grant it any importance to others as the real motivation for their ideas and actions, mostly align themselves with the social sciences in order for these to bestow upon what they are doing some sort of intellectual respectability.

Other religionists, for whom the importance of personal faith (not just, and certainly not mainly, their own, but that of most people) is an important part of understanding religion, are less keen to be embraced by what can seem to be a Judas-kiss of the soft sciences. For them, religion is a humane discipline, and the arts and humanities better house its content and its concerns. For them religion, at its most interesting and powerful, is a product of the disciplined imagination, in response to transcendent reality. To be sure, the social sciences can cast useful light upon religion, but it is a reflected light, and what it illuminates is of secondary importance. Sociology, psychology and cognate disciplines provide the framework within which, and secondary explanations of why, faith and action can flourish, for good and ill. But the social sciences do not exhaust the meaning, power and importance of religion, and their explanations are not the most interesting and sometimes not the most reasonable ones.

Uses of the word 'science', in contexts other than those of the natural sciences, are customarily regarded as historically valid, so long as they describe an organized body of knowledge that can be taught objectively. Many contemporary scholars of religion or religious studies who take shelter with social scientists no doubt feel that beneath the reassuring canopy of sacred 'facts' and 'objectivity' they are free from the suspicion that they are studying a subjective, irrational and disreputable topic, such as they are convinced religion must be when examined by people of faith. However, they may find that the canopy leaks. The term 'social science' first appeared in a book published in

1824 by William Thompson: *An Inquiry into the Principles of the Distribution of Wealth Most Conducive to Human Happiness; applied to the Newly Proposed System of Voluntary Equality of Wealth*. The father of sociology, Auguste Comte (d. 1857) argued that ideas pass through three rising stages, theological, philosophical and scientific. The first was rooted in assumption, the second in critical thinking, and the third in positive observation. So far, so interesting: though this is only a theory, and not one that is rooted in hard facts. The claims of social scientists to 'scientific' objectivity should not go unchallenged.

In fact, many early, and some not so early, social scientists were far from objective in their aims. The Englishman James Hunt, President of the newly formed Anthropological Society, observed in 1863, amid all the brouhaha about Darwin's theory of the origin of species:

> That the Negro is a different species from the European; that the analogies are far more numerous between the Negro and the ape than between the European and the ape; that the Negro is inferior intellectually to the European; that the Negro can only be humanized and civilized by Europeans.[9]

When these ugly words were spewed out, civil war was raging in the USA, partly over the issue of slavery. Hunt can be seen as a not very subtle advocate and partisan of the southern states. His was not an 'objective' statement, based upon sound evidence. Indeed, many nineteenth- and twentieth-century anthropologists worked in the vanguard of the British and other imperial projects, and some were its paid agents.

Other social sciences, too, were far from objective. Karl Marx's views of religion had a wide influence in the twentieth century, during the waxing and waning of communism. For him, religious life is symptomatic of unfulfilled human existence. Religion is where people achieve, in fantasy, what they do not have in reality: love, dignity, honour, and so forth. The idea of God expresses the reality of social alienation. In his most famous words: 'Religion is the sob of the oppressed creature, the heart of a heartless world, and the soul of soulless conditions. It is the opium of the people.' Marx was not speaking of religion as a human addiction, though it has certainly proved to be so. He was thinking of its drug-like properties of easing pain in ways that do nothing to improve the social and economic conditions that caused the pain. For Marx, religion therefore connives at grave injustice, and has no place in a well-ordered society: once social ills are redressed, religion will wither away. For all the impressive if wearisome scientific analyses of Marx, he was deeply indebted to Feuerbach's strongly held conviction that 'God is nothing else than man: he is, so to speak, the outward projection of man's inward nature.' This conviction was itself a derivation from Hegel's speculative theology. Speculative is the appropriate word. Marx has, of course, proven a false, or, if charity prevails, a minor, prophet. Ironically, the end of oppressive Marxist rule was greatly helped in Eastern Europe by a current of religious protest against social and economic ills. Some Marxists have understandably claimed that major communist powers and their individual rulers simply used Marx inappropriately to further their own selfish and very different ends. Quite so. A friendly Christian criticism of Marx's analysis of human society is that it lacks any notion or understanding of original sin, which is, when sensibly interpreted, a core and compelling Christian conviction about human nature. At the root of all Marx's impressive theory is, in practice, the assumption that humans (or, at least, working-class humans) will mostly behave in a sporting way towards one another if the economic conditions are sorted out as Marx recommends. No doubt, Marx's misplaced nineteenth-century faith in the inevitable progress of humanity explains this touchingly curious misreading of human nature, which had such lamentable consequences for a century and more after his death in 1883.

Maybe, though, it is not necessary to have a traditional view of religions and their accounts of humanity's sinful or un-enlightened state in order to plumb the depths of human nature. Perhaps a secular reading can offer a much better explanation. Sigmund Freud, a giant figure in the emerging discipline of psychology, certainly thought so. In his *Totem and Taboo* (1913), he located the roots of religion in the Oedipus complex, the repressed sexual desire for the mother by a male child, who is in conflict with his father for her favour. (According to a Greek myth, Oedipus unintentionally killed his father Laius and married his mother Jocasta.) Freud came to believe that the murder of a father within a primal horde really happened, that this act of parricide was repressed, and that religion preserves the memory of it. No wonder then that Freud saw religion as about neuroses and guilt. In *The Future of an Illusion* (1927), he condemned religion as something we can outgrow. By the end of his life, in *Moses and Monotheism* (1939), he interpreted the religion of Moses as a revival of the failed attempts of the Egyptian Pharaoh Amenhotep IV (who changed his name to Akhenaten) to enforce the worship of one God, depicted as the Aten, the disc of the sun. Moses was murdered by his followers after he led them to freedom, and the rise of Jewish (and, derivatively, Christian and Islamic) monotheism is linked to this murder. If others had come to Freud with his own theories of religious origins, he might have wanted to quiz them about this unhealthy obsession with primordial deaths in the family. Be that as it may, for Freud the Jewish belief in one God was not given through a divine revelatory act or acts, but is a neurotic symptom of this repressed murder, which struggles through the subconscious to appear, for example, in the teachings of the prophets. The usefulness of all this material for psychoanalytic theory and practice is for others to determine. It cannot, however, be claimed to be based upon any kind of 'objective' scholarship. Freud located events in the past, including pre-historic times, that historians, working patiently with the available data, have completely overlooked, for the excellent reason that there is no evidence for them. And, as Jung and other later practitioners of Freud's discipline pointed out, religion can have positive effects upon human thought and behaviour, which Freud completely disallowed.

One could continue to have some fun at the expense of early social scientists, many of whom mistook confused fanciful theory for evidence-based fact. Their contemplations arose within an atmosphere of a belief in inevitable human progress, to which many were convinced 'traditional' religion could not contribute, since it was often politically reactionary, socially repressive, and academically unrespectable. The fact that their own theories were far-fetched and unprovable, and were for the most part earnestly delivered with neither wit nor humour, did not trouble them at all. Of course, eminent exponents of the social sciences these days have more than made up for their originators' somewhat cavalier attitude to the facts. Outsiders to their world of discourse cannot but be impressed by the ponderous detail and elaborate methodology that goes into the constructions of, for example, much contemporary sociology.

Sceptics did not have the religious field open just to themselves. Victorian England and Scotland produced scholars of religion who may not have been conventional believers but who were interested in rescuing the possibility that religion may have something important to say about faith and belief and practices. Let the great Max Müller be our example. He paid religion the compliment of assuming that it might reflect some sort of positive reality rather than a foolish delusion or illusion. He coined the impressive phrase 'the scientific study of religion' in 1867 and clearly attempted to ground his studies in an 'objective' evaluation of the evidence. German by birth (his father produced minor poetry that Franz Schubert set to sublime music), he moved to England in 1848 and eventually became Professor of Comparative Philology at Oxford University. He lived out his love for India in the Bodleian and British Libraries, translating an edition of the Rig-Veda and 29 volumes of *Sacred Books of the East* (1879–94). He also translated Immanuel Kant's *Critique of Pure Reason* in 1891, and was in fact a Kantian Idealist, believing that, although the existence of God cannot be proven, we are led to believe 'through pure reason' that intelligible unities such as God, freedom and immortality do exist, and that these are practicable necessities for human living. Müller resisted the widespread assumption that humans develop from a primitive origin to more advanced stages. In his later years, he was a member of the Church of England, which he thought gave to its members greater freedom and more 'immunity from priestcraft' than any other religion. Despite his startlingly unusual tribute to England's established church, Müller was inclined to think that original religion in its purest form developed in India, where he is greatly and rightly honoured to this day. However, he never went to India and if he had done so would no doubt have condemned some of its practices as sad fallings-away from the beauty and power of original Hinduism. His aphorism about religions, that 'he who knows one knows none', found in his *Introduction to the Science of Religion* (1873), has much force. Still, he had little if any experiential understanding of other religions. Unlike him, most people do not work and live out their faith and beliefs in libraries. A number of university departments of religion quote this aphorism on their web sites, but it is doubtful whether they would want just head-knowledge of religion for their students. One hopes not.

Whither the study of religion?

For the most part, contemporary scholars have given up a quest for the origins of religion. Social scientists have settled instead for accounting for religion as it impacts their particular discipline in different ways. There are also some interesting hybrid disciplines: in many colleges and universities, you will find lecturers in the psychology of religion or the sociology of religion.

The discipline of Religious Studies remains something of a battleground. For some of its scholars, to use their kind of language: theology should not be privileged in the study of religion; or, faith infects the discourse, so should be confined to theological colleges (where, presumably, very ill people can be kept in isolation).

It is certainly true that some universities in the USA, founded and funded by conservative Christians who shun careful and reflective thinking, do not always create a community of scholars and a home where careful and reflective learning can flourish. Even so, such dismissive, weasel words about theology and faith often mask very questionable assumptions. Our brief trawl through the theories about religion of some early and distinguished social scientists has given the lie to any claims to their objectivity or any demonstrably scientific investigation.

The possibility of complete objectivity is one of modernity's more imperialistic assumptions, just as the impossibility of making wiser and better and truer choices than others is one of postmodernity's sillier suppositions. Objectivity is more of a quest than a clearly definable reality. All seekers after knowledge have to make allowances for personal preferences and even prejudices; and some succeed more than others. The idea that contemporary scholars of religion allow their personal convictions to intrude upon their findings, more often and more inappropriately than other academics do, is false. There are many scholars in other branches of learning whose commitment to a particular view of things gets in the way of an impartial assessment of the evidence, so some (by no means all) theologians are not the only academics who must plead guilty as charged.

Furthermore, the argument that scientific evidence must account for religion as something other than being about belief in a transcendent reality is a presupposition and not a logical necessity. To most scholars in many times and places, it would seem a questionable, even a foolish, conjecture. The twentieth-century Methodist minister Lord Soper used to observe that the knowledge of God surpasses human understanding, it does not bypass it. Religious scholars have usually, except when they have lost their confidence as well as faith in their subject, prized reason but also argued for the limitations of reason. Other factors are necessary in order to follow truth wherever it may lead: among them, revelation and various responses to it. The first universities were founded in North Africa and Europe as religious institutions. Some attempted to bring reason and revelation together in a fruitful dialogue. Al-Azhar in Egypt was founded under the heterodox Fatamid Islamic dynasty towards the end of the tenth century CE, though it soon became Sunni Islam's premier centre of learning; and universities flourished in France and England from the twelfth century onwards. Older than any other university is the University of al-Qarawiyin in Morocco, founded in 859 and a centre of Sunni Islamic higher learning ever since.

Some of the current crop of scholars who condemn religion as inherently unreasonable and violent do not themselves apply careful reasoning to their subject. Richard Dawkins, for example, does not consider any evidence that contradicts his assertions about religion, nor does he pause to consider the multi-faceted lives, beliefs and practices of religious people. Still, because others play fast and loose with data does not mean that religionists should do likewise. As St Paul might have observed, we should show them a better way.

Just as our understanding of what constitutes objectivity has changed, so it is possible to argue that our methods of ordering and understanding knowledge have also changed, or should have. In his witty and wise book on the historian's craft, John Lewis Gaddis expresses his puzzlement with the entrenched ways of contemporary social scientists, and their obsession with distinguishing independent from dependent variables. He records being at a conference and asking a group of them: 'How, apart from God if he or she exists, can there ever be such a thing as an independent variable? Aren't all variables dependent on other variables?' He received only blank looks and, from the chair, after a pause, the words 'Well, moving right along . . .'.[10] Social scientists, Gaddis argues, work with a reductionist view of reality, searching for the element whose removal from a causal chain would alter the outcome. This might make sense in mathematics or a laboratory, but it no longer works as the way of making sense of many of the natural sciences (or, of course, of the humanities). Not every scientific event can be reproduced in a laboratory. Geologists can tell us a great deal about the centre of the earth though nobody has ever drilled more than a few miles deep. Astronomers map the far places of the universe from within the earth's orbit. Gaddis concludes:

> The search for independent variables in the social sciences can't succeed because the procedures upon which it depends are based on an outmoded view of the so-called 'hard' sciences. Social scientists during the twentieth century embraced a Newtonian vision of linear and therefore predictable phenomena even as the natural sciences were abandoning it. Hence, the methodological passing of ships in the night.[11]

If religionists could regain their nerve, they might take a leaf or two out of Gaddis' book. He aligns the study of history more closely, in its methods, to the evolutionary than the social sciences: 'both history and the evolutionary sciences practice the remote sensing of phenomena with which they can never directly interact'.[12] Well, the study of religion is not quite history, though it is more like history than maths or biology. It does not have to act as though it were a social science in order to gain academic respectability. It might come out from under a great pile of often-irrelevant and torpor-inducing methodological jargon, and formulate its own place as a respectable discipline, if some of its academics had the nerve to see through the emperor's new clothes it is presently wrapped in (or not, as the case may be). The same might actually be claimed for the social sciences. For too long, their advocates have modelled their ways of verifying their data, and even justifying their subjects, on a really quite shaky and now rather passé analogy with the ways that harder, natural sciences handle (or, in many cases, used to handle) their evidence.

It is not my intention in this book to construct new and more appropriate methodologies of religion, still less to make life easier for my colleagues in the social sciences. In fact, much useful methodological work has been done for the study of religion in the last 30 years or so by such excellent and eminent scholars as Ninian Smart, Ursula King and Frank Whaling, to whose achievements we shall turn in due course. Rather, it is my intention to reinforce and elaborate the obvious which, for a variety of reasons, stopped being obvious for a while.

Religion, for most people, is about transcendent reality. It cannot be denied that Marx and Freud and other notable social scientists of their day and since have alerted us to ways in which religion can be used as a tool of political oppression, or show itself in mental illness or in some other unhealthy or even wicked way. It can also, as many other scholars of the social sciences have shown, contribute to human wellbeing. But, if these are some of the effects of religion, we can still ask: what is the heart of religion? What is religion for? Religion is a quest for truth. It relies upon the conviction that life's meanings are not exhausted by the physical senses: there is more to life than meets the eye. If so, then despite all its vicissitudes in the modern world theology may still prove to be the queen of sciences, offering hope and meaning in a fallen world.

3

Living Religion Today

Outsiders who examine the concerns of many contemporary scholars of religious studies could be forgiven for thinking that religion is primarily an object to be examined and categorized. This might surprise them, given that, for most of the world's history (and maybe prehistory), religion has been lived, not pigeon-holed. Most people have not bothered to examine it overmuch, but have simply accepted it as a way of making sense of life. Of course, scholars need to interpret the data of religion. Nevertheless, living religion today resists any easy organization and definition.

A mess of religious potage

Many years ago, I was a very part-time hospital chaplain in London. To be precise, I was Free Church chaplain. In practice, I was often asked to see any patients who had not registered themselves as Anglican or Roman Catholic on the part of the hospital admissions form marked 'religion'. Both hospitals to which I was attached confused religion with denomination. They are not alone in this. I have usually thought of myself as living out of Christian faith or, if pressed, have identified myself as a member of the Christian religion; but I long ago became resigned to admitting to Methodism whenever someone asks the common but spectacularly inaccurate question: 'So what religion do you belong to, vicar?'

In late-1970s London, hospitals determined that religion was a choice: an institution to which one belonged or did not belong. To be sure, I met plenty of people who were ardent members of Methodist, Baptist or United Reformed churches, some of whom had a disturbing tendency to define themselves over against another denominational option, asserting, for example, that 'Catholics aren't real Christians'. Yet as often as not I sat and talked with people who had long before given up on institutional religion, or who had never belonged to any 'religion'. They would often tell me why the institutional Church was not for them, sometimes defensively with an eye to my clerical collar, but more often in a matter-of-fact way. Nevertheless, some would tell me of their life of faith outside any denominational commitment, occasionally to impress me, but mostly because faith meant a great deal to them, not least in helping them make sense of their situation as they talked with me in the shadow of illness and sometimes of death. I had some memorable moments: a dying man wanted to be married by a parson to his much-younger partner ('Would you do this for us, vicar?'), and intended to 'get it right this time', for she would be his fifth wife; and, when I nodded off to sleep while listening to a woman a few days away from death, she responded humorously and with gentle irony, 'You need it more than I do.' Both these people had not lost faith or hope or love, and neither of them thought that to stroke a crystal or follow some charismatic figure in a new sect was a better alternative to attending morning worship at Wesley's Chapel or some other imposing edifice of the institutional Church. Some sociologists would describe them as believing, not belonging. But surely it was more of a case of having faith, but not belonging to *the* or *a* faith. Many such people wanted me to pray with and for them.

In the summer of 1985, I spent two weeks in a small, remote village in the Punjab province of Pakistan. I did not go as an anthropologist, to study the behavioural patterns and group relations of its residents. Nor did I go as the sort of Christian theologian or missiologist who would be determined to expound Christian ideas of God to anyone who would listen. I went in order to improve my knowledge of Urdu, which was one of the two languages spoken there. At the time I was a circuit minister, so it was natural for me to be curious about people's faith and practice, and equally natural for them to wonder what a Christian clergyman was doing in their midst. All this led to intriguing and illuminating and quite unplanned conversations. I soon detected one obvious difference from my experiences in London: in this Pakistani village, religion was not perceived by any institution or person as a choice. It was assumed to be a natural dimension within everyday life. My experiences in the village taught me that when religion becomes a 'thing', there is a tendency to over-exaggerate what you have to believe and do in order to belong; whereas when it is a dimension within society, as it is there, people express their religious selves in rather unselfconscious ways. For example: when most teachers expound Islam, they point out that Sunni Muslims pray five times a day, as prescribed by religious law; yet in that village, men (sometimes mildly pestered by their mothers and wives) and women all gathered for the Friday lunchtime prayers, but prayed at other prescribed times when they remembered, or felt like it, or not at all. In talking to some of those whose commitment to religious practices seemed minimal, I found no actual or budding atheists. Everyone took it for granted that there was a sacred canopy overarching their lives. I was reminded of Wilfred Cantwell Smith's point that there is a cumulative tradition of faith (in that village, Islamic faith), which people draw from as they wish and as they are able. Even in religions of law, theoretically requiring obedience to Sharia obligations or to 613 *mitzvot* or commandments, in practice most people draw upon such requirements in a less formal and totalitarian way in order to construct and live out their lives of faith. This is not the 'pick and mix' practice of the contemporary West, but a natural and instinctive way of being, in the case of those villagers, Muslim. To put it in a slightly exaggerated way: religion there exists for people, not vice versa.

The women nagged their menfolk about faith somewhat, but they did so affectionately and they did not have to push too hard to make them willing to pray and do good deeds, at least on an occasional basis. It is important to emphasize that people were not bullied into being faithful Muslims, under threat of social ostracism or some other sanction. They just were who they were. The local imam, who looked after the mosque and taught children enough Arabic to pray, was treated with warmth and respect, but his religious rulings were not accepted unquestioningly. One man wanted to show me the tomb of his mother, but the imam told him that it was not fit for me, as a foreigner, to visit the graveyard. We left but came back when he had gone away. I started to ask if it was the right thing to do to disobey the imam, but the words faltered on my lips when I saw the twinkle in my new friend's eye.

During my short time there, I found myself influenced by this rather different way of living religion (premodern, if one wishes to use western jargon, though that can seem insufferably condescending). The most obvious example occurred on an occasion when I left the village for the day. I started my return journey rather late, and found that I was stranded after nightfall at a small railway station some considerable distance short of the village. It was dark and deserted, there were bandits in the area, and I should have been afraid. Instead, I assumed that the universe was a friendly place, found myself telling God that my future was in his hands, and hoped for a good outcome. I remember feeling content. After some time a horse and trap appeared from nowhere, and took me on a long and bumpy ride to the nearest village to my own where I happened upon a man with whom I had previously struck up a conversation. He offered me a bed for the night, but drove me back to where I was staying when I expressed the desire to get there before I was missed.

I have never been a great fan of the idea that God provides car parking spaces to those particularly faithful people who are in need of them, an opinion I used to express forcefully, several years later, to shallow seminarians who thought he owed them that privilege. I could make a case for his intervention for me in Pakistan on the grounds that, unlike them, I did not feel entitled to God's help, and that I was in direr straits than someone trying to get her car as close as possible to the supermarket entrance. Yet that only explains one set of problems in order to raise others. Looking back, I was possibly foolish or addled. One thing, though: I knew then as I know now that my hope for a safe end to my predicament was not the certainty of it, that I was in a mess of my own making, and that it might have bad consequences for me. Knowing that, I still felt content. Another way of living religion had taken me over. Probably, this new perspective is best described as an old one, rediscovered; one that takes God and faith for granted as sources of help and of hope, and sees the limitations of reason. If you always have to explain the point of religion, you might just explain it away or never get to the stage where you simply trust in God's mercy and compassion.

This perspective was not to be precisely identified with Islam, though its form in Pakistan was Muslim. In India or Africa, and other places, it could be Hindu or Christian or primal or some other expression of faith that provided a similar way of being religious and faithful. As for myself, that day I felt what I felt as a Christian, and it was to the Father of Jesus that I spoke in expectation and prayer. But I was indebted to Muslims for showing me how I could do so.

It is not a persuasive argument that acquiring such a new perspective on faith is simply to do with copying what you see; still less is it accurate to suppose, as some anthropologists and phenomenologists of religion do, that an empathetic understanding of others is always a positive stance and will inevitably rub off on the participant observer. Empathy is not all that it is cracked up to be: it is a neutral quality, to be used well or ill. One of the most empathetic characters in English literature is Iago, who insinuates himself into the mind of Othello perfectly, in order to destroy him. In spite of that alarming example, it has become quite the thing in some interfaith and study of religion circles to talk positively and often uncritically about insider and outsider perspectives, to assume that it is a constructive and affirmative thing to make the transition from the latter to the former, and to enquire how this can be done. Some religionists claim that the knowledge of a language, or attachment to a partner of another faith or culture, or both, gives them heaps of empathy, and honorary insider status. Some live out their dialogical experiences through the world-wide web, in virtual reality, where for them relationships seem easier to make, sustain and interpret as being 'insider' than many of us have found them to be, face to face. Their smugness and naïveté will not do. Arguably, theirs is just another modernist tendency to classify people glibly and inappropriately. In reality, I am not a Pakistani villager, I am conditioned by what I have been and done, and who I am (white and male and British and middle-class). At most, I can claim that such things as my years in India and that two-week sojourn in a Punjabi village have broadened and deepened and enriched who I am. And I can also be glad, along with all people of goodwill, that, despite all the divisions of race, culture, language and religion, enough is shared in common by most humans to make encounters hopeful and joyful and loving. It is certainly the case that actual meetings with real people complicate ideas and conditions, delightfully.

Critics would argue that what I have described is clear-cut irrationality, the bane of all religious thought and belief. Most people, being religious, would counter, with Pascal, that 'the heart has its reasons, whereof reason knows nothing'; or, more prosaically, that there is more to a discerning life than the exercise of reason. But this perspective is not just to do with being more or less reasonable. It is to do with recognizing that religion can be a dimension in life that one takes for granted and not just a denominational or institutional or any other sort of choice.

Or, to put it differently, we live in a world in which the most important religious choices are not the ones we make. Klaus Klostermaier, a Christian living for two years in one of the holiest places in north India, made friends with a 74-year-old man, Gopalji, a devotee of Lord Krishna. Mindful no doubt of India's multitude of deities, Klostermaier once said to him, 'Is it not presumptuous to choose one's own Ishtadevta, the God one adores?'

'It is not we who choose our God, it is our God who chooses us,' he replied.[1]

Just so.

Contemporary interpretations of religion

It would be possible to yearn, sentimentally, for a vision of the religious past that would make sense of a difficult present for religion in Europe; possible, but pointless. We cannot completely 'unthingify' religion, and return it to what we may consider a purer form. We have to live religion as it is, and seek to improve it, if we are to be faithful in relevant ways.

My experiences of hospital chaplaincy in London now suggest to me that, although Europeans tend to categorize religion and turn it into a choice, for many it also remains a dimension in society to which they turn in hope and need, just as it is in that Pakistani village. Many Europeans may not have chosen to identify with a particular denomination, but they draw upon aspects of Christian faith to sustain them. It would be possible to dismiss them as cultural or residual Christians, but that would miss the point.

The process of globalization also means that many people in Asia, Africa and elsewhere have come to regard religion as, to some extent and rather more sharply than once they did, an object of choice, with relatively clearly defined boundaries. One result of making it such a choice is that some of them regard other, even quite similar, choices as sharply and culpably differentiated from their own. As I write these words, a group of Sunni Muslim terrorists has just blown up minarets of a mosque in Iraq that is holy to Shia Muslims; indeed, Iraq is in a state of civil war in which Sunni and Shia Islam (and even different shades of Sunni and Shia 'membership') have become badges of competing identities. Tensions have long existed between believers who practise these two different ways of being Muslim, but they have been exacerbated by globalization: fundamentalist Muslims have learned, to a great extent from western thought and practice, to turn their faith into a tightly boundaried 'thing' and to describe that 'thing' in narrow and excluding ways. It is but a short step further to feel comfortable about marginalizing and even destroying Muslims who hold different religious views than their own.

Ayman al-Zawahiri is notorious in the West as a prominent member and spokesman of al-Qaida and its campaign against America and its allies; he is sometimes described as its second-in-command. Zawahiri certainly has western 'crusader' nations in his sights, and also Israel. He asserts that the first stage in ridding the Middle East of false interpretations of Islam and of the state of Israel is forcing Americans out of Iraq. In the wake of President Bush's proposal in January 2007 to send a surge of 20,000 more American troops to Iraq, al-Zawahiri released a video in which he said that 'Iraq . . . is able to bury ten armies like yours, with God's help and power.' He is perhaps less well known for his hate-filled utterances against interpretations of Islam that do not agree with his own. A Sunni Muslim himself (though with a narrow and trivial understanding of that Muslim way), he regards the Shia interpretation of Islam as 'a religious school based on excess and falsehood'. He has proven willing, in the short term, to foster Shia support against the USA and its allies, though his long-term aim is the establishment of a

Sunni *Dar al-Islam* (territories governed by Muslim Sharia law) over as wide an area as possible, which he realizes would inevitably lead to a conflict with Shia-majority Iran and other Shia Muslims. He is also dismissive of Sunni Muslims who disagree with him, and is willing insouciantly to countenance their death to further his own objectives. This partisan of a bigoted interpretation of Islam, conversant in English and French as well as Arabic, a lover of poetry, and once a student of psychology and pharmacology at Cairo University, is far more indebted to western thought than most Europeans and Americans realize. And, ironically, his distorted interpretation of Islam is far more indebted to western thought and specifically to its objectification of religion than he realizes.

Because the European faith that Enlightenment thinkers objectified was overwhelmingly the Christian faith, it was widely assumed, indeed taken for granted, by these thinkers that all religious systems had (or should have) scriptures, priests, doctrines, and all the other appurtenances of important branches of the Christian faith. When the European imperial enterprise got under way in Asia and Africa, in the eighteenth century and afterwards, other non-Christian ways of faith were similarly objectified and forced onto a western template; this, even though Hindu and Buddhist faith and what (much later, in the 1950s) came to be called African Traditional Religion were deeply woven into the fabric of society, and were not separate voluntary or charitable organizations. The modern European reflex habit of making religion a 'thing', coupled with imperial *hauteur*, meant that many colonial officials and missionaries had a distorted and judgemental interpretation of what they saw. There was much scope for misunderstanding, the legacy of which has persisted down to our own times.

A particularly notable example of misplaced colonial categorization and condescension is the reaction of British people to South Asian ways of faith they encountered. The word 'Hindu' had been used in a geographical sense of people who lived in what is now, roughly, India, way back in the first millennium BCE by Greeks and Persians. The use of 'Hindu' to refer to a religious person can be dated to Chinese references in the seventh century CE. Muslims used it in this way from the following century onwards, and Europeans from the early seventeenth century. These depictions made some sense, though it is a good principle to listen to people's self-definitions more carefully than to those of outsiders. However, to turn Hindu faith and practice into a system within which Hindus live was, in some important ways, a false step. Yet, in spite of the fact that Indian faith was bewilderingly diverse, British observers did exactly that: they forced related families of faith into a single uniform 'Hinduism', a term that, so far as we can tell, was first written down in the 1780s. An intriguing result of the European arrangement of other families of faith is that they began to persuade others of the merits of their assumption, including those whose ways of faith they were imperfectly judging and classifying. For example, three decades after Charles Grant referred to 'Hindooism' in a letter written in 1787, the Bengali Indian Hindu reformer, Rammohun Roy, did so in 1816 and again in 1817.

Other Europeans working in the colonial period offered categorizations that were far more affirmative and appreciative of the faith that they encountered. The distinguished British Methodist minister Geoffrey Parrinder, who died in 2005 but who had much earlier worked in West Africa for most of the period from 1933 to 1956, built on the work of the Primitive Methodist minister and anthropologist Edwin Smith to construct an interpretation of West African religion. He noted, across a wide number of West African peoples: belief in a high god; belief in lower gods; belief in divinized ancestors; and charms and amulets. By 1954, Parrinder had extended this depiction of African Traditional Religion, in a book of that name, to cover all of sub-Saharan Africa. He saw African Traditional Religion as one of Africa's three living religions, along with Christianity and Islam. Before that, many European scholars of African primal faith had dismissed it as primitive and superstitious. Parrinder's classification gave to Africans, even those who converted to Christianity or Islam, a means of valuing their ancestral faith. Intriguingly, although Parrinder taught and wrote widely about Indian religion, he never extended his insights about African primal faiths to the South Asian context. A case could be made that the enormous varieties of Indian faith subsumed under the modern creation of Hinduism could be more appropriately categorized as Indian Traditional Religion, though using a different classification than the fourfold model that Parrinder discerned among African peoples. He was careful to describe that fourfold categorization as 'a working classification', meaning that it was a useful tool until something better came along. Certainly, most Africanists would now want to refine his model, but it has worn surprisingly well, and influenced most scholars of African religion since, even those who do not acknowledge their indebtedness to his work.

It is possible to classify religion helpfully or unhelpfully, condescendingly or constructively. These classifications can be appropriated and reworked, or else rejected, by those who are the object of them.

What, however, about ways of classifying, not just a group of religions (as they are perceived by the classifier) but religion as a whole? At the turn of the twentieth century, Baron von Hügel argued that religion can be divided into institutional, intellectual and mystical. This typology, in his view, conveyed the tension and 'friction' that exists in religion. It is indeed a useful basic classification, but others since have greatly refined it and produced other categories. Ninian Smart has proposed seven dimensions of a religion: practical and ritual; experiential and emotional; narrative or mythic; doctrinal and philosophical; ethical and legal; social and institutional; and the material.[2] Frank Whaling offered this similar approach:

. . . all the major religions of the world contain eight inter-linked elements. The major religions are dynamic organisms within which there are eight interacting dimensions; they are historical chains within which there are eight connecting links. The eight links are those of religious community, ritual, ethics, social involvement, scripture/myth, concepts, aesthetics and spirituality. All religions have some sort of religious community, they all engage in different forms of worship, lying behind them are certain ethical norms, they are all involved in social and political outreach within the wider community, sacred texts and myths are important for them all, they all emphasise particular clusters of doctrines, they all produce religious art and sculpture, and they all infer distinctive modes of spirituality. In other words there are eight common elements within the great world religions and it is a great help to be aware of this for they provide pegs upon which knowledge can be hung.[3]

Such classifications are useful teaching aids. It can be quite instructive and amusing to point out to a conservative evangelical Christian student that it is not just her reading of Scripture that differs from that of a Roman Catholic, but also the relative importance she gives to the Bible within a range of artefacts, thought and behaviours that shape different expressions of Christian faith; and vice versa. Such classifications can help students to see beyond their own perceptions to greater riches from which they can draw to refine and extend their own narrow understanding of ultimate reality. Would that Ayman al-Zawahiri (and Pat and Osama from the opening of chapter 1) could understand that life's complexities demand a variety of religious responses rather than simplistic, trivial and immoral certainties.

Religion is not a uniform thing. It cannot be reduced to a manageable set of beliefs and practices. To do so runs the risk of trivializing religion, even if with good intent. It has recently become quite the thing in interfaith circles to emphasize the golden rule as a shared value. As it happens, I am wearing a T-shirt just now that has written upon it that 'rule' as it is expressed in seven different faiths. Although it is delightful and important to know that we should treat our neighbours as ourselves, and shameful to admit that we find it so difficult to do, simple morality is not all that religion has to teach us. How does the golden rule cash out in terms of, for example, our attitudes to war and peace; our views about when life begins and ends; our attitudes to poverty and injustice? And surely we need to supplement the golden rule with other, more profound, ethical thinking. It is not clear, for example, that emphasizing the importance of treating others as you yourself would wish to be treated would make a significant contribution to the range and complexity of contemporary debates about the beginning and ending of human life.

Nor is religious meaning exhausted by rather more profound ethical reflection (or even action), useful though that can be. Religion is more than ethics. When King David danced naked with others before the ark of the Lord, his wife despised him, and we too might share her snobbish disdain for such (we might think) unnecessary and degrading practices. But David's divine Spirit-led abandonment to the moment was as much a religious act as was the stern moral judgement that he later faced from the prophet Nathan for his acts of adultery and murder (1 Samuel 6.16–23; 11—12.25). Religion troubles us into truth, by its many ways of touching the heart and the mind. Smart's and Whaling's and other models of religion encourage us to recognize and explore those many dimensions of religion.

However, it is important not to make any classification, however perceptive and subtle, more than an indication of the rich diversity of religion. Religions do not quite conform to any classification, however flexibly framed: primal faith, for example, mostly has no written scripture, though it does have wonderfully evocative stories.

The end of religion

Religious people are well aware of the importance of religion. A good Methodist may be on a number of church committees, support local and circuit causes, and attend innumerable acts of worship and ecumenical meetings. And so on. In fellowship with other members of the body of Christ, she may also find dimensions of life that support her in good times and bad, and help her construct the sort of person she aspires to be. Let us use the aforementioned eightfold model of Frank Whaling, himself a Methodist minister as well as a distinguished scholar of religious studies, to make this point. Our good Methodist may find in her religious community, and in the faith of others, inspiration to continue her own pilgrimage of faith. The rituals of church, too, provide her with a sense of belonging to something that extends back into the historical past, a link with people who, as an example, took bread and wine as we do, and for the same reason: to bring to mind the death and resurrection of the Lord Jesus. Thereby, she is also taken into a timeless and transcendent plane, beyond the sense experiences. She finds with other Methodists a meaningful and honourable way of life, among a group of people who seek to live out the values of God's kingdom, and whose care for each other provides a model for earthly societies as well as the divine commonwealth. Working with them and others in the wider community reminds her of God's presence in unlikely places and people. The stories of Jesus, and other Scripture passages, give her a sense of God's presence in mundane things. Core beliefs help her to understand the importance of Jesus and of God's mercy, power and love, and give some sort of shape and order and clarity to her interpretation of faith. Great art and music, and every now and then even a badly played harmonium or kitschy religious picture hanging on the chapel wall, can transport her to a place where divine things are accessible when prosy words fail. And all these things equip her to construct a life of faith that can be made relevant to, and possible within, her own busy schedule.

That, of course, is the desirable outcome. Doubtless, she will also find back-biting and gossip, and other somewhat human but rather unworthy responses to the promptings of the divine Spirit. Even these can prove a spur to improve oneself and an impetus to humour, forgiveness and other worthy qualities.

For many people, religion is an incomparably important dimension to life. So it is important that it be good religion and not bad. Religion as purveyed by such exponents as Ayman al-Zawahiri is bad religion, because it ignores many of the dimensions of religion that Smart, Whaling and others point to, and is therefore thin and bitter gruel to sustain a person's spiritual life. It also offers the dark side of the dimensions that it does engage with: for example, the ethical vision of al-Qaida is a distortion of classical Islamic teaching, offering, as it does, not a dream of human community but a nightmare of sectarian hatred.

Bad religion flourishes elsewhere than Islam, of course. Pat Robertson, national religious broadcaster and former USA presidential candidate, has a large following for his television talk show, *The 700 Club*. His views are racy and controversial. In early 2007, he told his listeners that God had revealed to him that a major terrorist attack would take place in the USA later that year, resulting in mass killing, though he hedged his bets about whether it would be nuclear. Americans could take heart from the fact that he and God have sometimes got their wires crossed, for his prophecies have not always been accurate. In 2004, he predicted that President Bush would easily win re-election – he squeezed in with 51 per cent of the vote – and in 2005 he maintained that Social Security reform would be approved in the USA – it was not. Many of Robertson's opinions, expressed with freedom and candour, have surprised their targets. For example, after a business deal with the Bank of Scotland broke down in 1999, due to his negative views about gays, Robertson gave it as his judgement that Scotland is 'a dark land overrun by homosexuals'. Other opinions have angered or embarrassed people. In August 2005, he suggested that the Venezuelan leader Hugo Chavez should be assassinated, leading the then US Defense Secretary Donald Rumsfeld to observe that 'our department doesn't do that kind of thing'. In response, Robertson offered a kind of apology. He has a history of kind of apologizing for some of his utterances. After the Israeli Prime Minister Ariel Sharon's massive stroke, he said in January 2006 that it could have been God's retribution for handing over Israeli land to the Palestinians. Following a public outcry, he apologized to Sharon's son.

Robertson's views have alienated many people of goodwill. Some have been at odds not just with him, but with religion itself, which they see as a cloak or justification for his utterances, and for the words and deeds of other immature, weak-minded or wicked people. They are also appalled by the fact that he can attract a significant following for exclusive and often hate-filled words. Not only are secular people revolted. Many religious practitioners also regard the faith of Pat Robertson and Ayman al-Zawahiri not only as pointlessly and aggressively exclusive but also as a dim and dismal distortion and trivialization of true religion.

Religion has many dimensions that, when appropriated for good and not for ill, can offer a lifetime of hope. Occasionally, however, scholars of religion seem to miss the wood for the trees, being so interested in the manifold forms of religious life that they miss what they are there for. Although religion is a multi-faceted network of beliefs, practices and other phenomena, for the most part, the most important sources of religions locate a primary emphasis. To put this another way and as a question: what is the heart of religion?

Different religions describe this 'heart' in different ways, and it is more accurate to point to a series of overlapping visionary cores of religion, not just a simple, one-sentence catechetical response. There is more to life than meets the eye, more than can be discerned by any of the senses, and wholesome religion is the means of our knowing and connecting to this truth. In describing this 'more', scholars of religion have often fallen into traps of their own making, assuming, for example, that belief in God is a common teaching of all religions. Yet some religions do not believe in a creator God; most schools of Buddhism for instance. The Buddha himself accepted the existence of supernatural beings or gods but thought them irrelevant to the process of human enlightenment.

The heart of all religious experience is trust in a transcendent element to life. Beyond the scan of the human senses lies a way that the world really works, to which those who understand this feel compelled to conform themselves. The religious life is how they do so. That transcendent dimension enables the fullness of life, a depth for the mind to explore and the heart to sing. Jesus called it the kingdom of God, a realm where God's will is done, partly on earth and fully in heaven. It is the divine commonwealth. The end of religion, in the sense of its purpose, is to enable people to access and live out of that dimension. For Christians and many other people of faith, unlike Buddhists and some others, the way to describe that transcendence is through God-language. Since this book is written from a Christian perspective, we shall refer to God, though we need to bear in mind that others will use different language.

Many scholars of religion, especially those wedded to the social sciences, are scandalized by what they see as this privileging of theology in the study of religion. For them, sociological or psychological or other entirely human explanations of religion make best sense of the data. Well, that is their opinion, often expressed in the earnest and complicated language of their disciplines. Others can see that it completely misses the point of religion. The English orchestral conductor Sir Thomas Beecham once observed that 'A musicologist is a man who can read music but can't hear it.' It would seem that theoreticians in a number of disciplines cannot see the wood for the trees, or hear the music of the spheres.

For most people, religion is about themselves in relation to transcendence. Sceptical scholars of religion may actually know better; or they may, for all their knowledge, be as useful and convincing as noisy but tone-deaf music critics. Theologians, namely, those who believe in that transcendent dimension and its importance in explaining what motivates people, are not necessarily prone to allow faith to shade the evidence of religious phenomena inappropriately. But they are right to take faith very seriously indeed, and to retort to some critics that for religionists not to do so is as weird as a mathematician who is forbidden or chooses not to deal with numbers.

Some contemporary critics of religion who contend that it is a human creation do so as though they and a few other secularly enlightened people are the first to notice this somewhat obvious and trivial point. On a number of pages of Christopher Hitchens' enjoyably abusive rant against religion, he describes it, scornfully, as man-made. Well, of course religion is. It uses human words to describe the ineffable. How else could it? Its liturgical actions, great buildings and artistic endeavours are the work of human hands. What else could they be? Its doctrines and beliefs are the constructs of human thought and of the human imagination. What is the alternative? If humans are to respond to the transcendent element to life, they have to use their mundane resources to do so. The question is not whether religion is a human creation; clearly it is. The issue is whether transcendent reality participates in the human process of engaging with it. In Christian terms, does God evoke responses from us, through forms that are available to us? Does religion enable a divine encounter with human beings?

Regrettably, it is often the case that religious people mistake the means for the end. Some Muslims who shout 'God is greater' seem to mean 'Islam is greater'. Many revivalist Hindus in India in the 1990s identified Muslims as the enemy, rather than God as their friend. Some American Jews are so uncritically pro-Israel as to forget the prophetic teaching to do justice

"Mr conspicuously omits the Bible from his list of human constructs, though admitting that it will eventually be lost in ultraviolet light."

The Churches'

Celebration Concert

for Christian Aid

with Hathern Band & Guest Soloists

Saturday 16th June 2007 at 7.30pm

Charnwood Road Baptist Church

– Admission £5 –

and to love mercy and to walk humbly with God. Some American Protestants associate their eccentric points of view with the clear teachings of Scripture, and so politicize religion inappropriately, with the help of foolish politicians who are not intelligent enough or else too arrogant to see that riding that tiger is destructive for them and for others. No wonder, then, that some thoughtful outsiders are put off religion by the self-serving actions of some of its devotees.

Still, for most people religion is still their means to the end of glorifying God and enjoying him for ever. That sentence is the language of the Westminster Shorter Catechism (1647); other religious people will find a variety of appropriate ways of making the same point about their commitment to transcendence, and its to them.

Yet, despite the importance of religion, it will come to an end when it has served its purpose. The Buddha described the *dhamma* (his teachings and the truths they contain) using the simile of a raft. The *dhamma* is like a raft, carrying a person over the ocean of birth and death. When a person arrives at the far shore, he might decide to carry the raft on his head because of its former usefulness to him. That would be absurd, for it has served its purpose and can be let go. The Buddhist teaching on non-attachment applies even to the *dhamma*.

The author of the book of Revelation makes a similar point. In his description of the holy city, the new Jerusalem, coming down out of heaven from God, adorned like a bride for her husband, he records that 'I saw no temple in the city, for its temple is the Lord God the Almighty and the Lamb' (21.22). In the life of heaven, there will be no need for religion and its artefacts (Temple or Bible or whatever), for then we shall see and know and serve God, and find our consummation in his love. The Second Temple in the earthly Jerusalem had been destroyed by the Romans in 70 CE, probably about 25 years before John of Patmos wrote these words. Roman pagans had looted and destroyed the central shrine of Jewish faith. John knew that all that seems secure and invulnerable in religion can come to an end. He also knew that God's goodness is not destroyed thereby.

John's vision of the new Jerusalem makes many allusions to Old Testament passages. Perhaps the most poignant is to the opening chapters of Genesis, and its description of divine creation, human failure, and the promise of redemption. John depicts how human sin, described at the beginning of the Bible, will be overcome in a new creation. Some greying Methodists will remember singing a rather sentimental hymn (number 857) from *The Methodist Hymn Book* of 1933 that began:

> God has given us a Book full of stories
> Which was made for his people of old.
> It begins with the tale of a garden
> And ends with the city of gold.

Between these two mythic acts of creation, humans live the life of faith, sustained by religion. In the new Jerusalem, faith will be swallowed up in knowledge. The purpose of the Temple will be achieved, for then we shall see God face to face. That is the end of religion, and, when it is fulfilled, religion will end.

To a poet a thousand years hence

> I who am dead a thousand years,
> And write this sweet archaic song,
> Send you my words for messengers
> The way I shall not pass along.
>
> I care not if you bridge the seas,
> Or ride secure the cruel sky,
> Or build consummate palaces
> Of metal or of masonry.

But have you wine and music still,
And statues and a bright-eyed love,
And foolish thoughts of good and ill,
And prayers to them that sit above?

How shall we conquer? Like a wind
That falls at eve our fancies blow,
And old Maeonides the blind[4]
Said it three thousand years ago.

O friend unseen, unborn, unknown,
Student of our sweet English tongue,
Read out my words at night, alone:
I was a poet, I was young.

Since I can never see your face,
And never shake you by the hand,
I send my soul through time and space
To greet you. You will understand.

The twentieth-century English composer Gerald Finzi set these words of James Elroy Flecker to music. Towards the end of his life (he died young of non-Hodgkins lymphoma) Finzi wrote, echoing Flecker's thought:

> I like to think that in each generation may be found a few responsive minds . . . To shake hands with a good friend over the centuries is a pleasant thing, and the affection which an individual may retain after his departure is perhaps the only thing which guarantees an ultimate life to his works.[5]

Flecker himself died young in 1915, of tuberculosis. He wrote sentimentally and exotically of the Orient: his poems 'The Gates of Damascus' and 'The Golden Journey to Samarkand' were once popular; as was his play *Hassan*, for which another English composer, Frederick Delius, wrote incidental music.

Flecker's words touch on something important to religion as well as acknowledged by poets, musicians and other artists. Religious people are caught up in a web of meaning that stretches through time and space. Christians are linked to the life and meaning of Jesus of Nazareth, and to all who have tried to make sense of and live by what God did and said through him. And, since he himself was indebted to God's covenant relationship with his Jewish people, Christians are linked back beyond Jesus to our father Abraham and mother Sarah, and farther back again to stories of Adam and Eve. Tradition is important to religions, as anyone who has seen the musical *Fiddler on the Roof* should know!

Religion links people across time, at its best, by faith and hope and love and other virtues. One fine day, time will dissolve into eternity and religion will come to an end, having served its purpose. Until then, it brings people to God. Or does it?

Religion has recently come under attack not only from outsiders but also from insiders, who feel threatened and marginalized by some of its forms. Such internal criticisms have always been a part of religion, a point which some contemporary insiders seem to have forgotten or never to have known. Some of them are too eager to abandon the past, as though it were a virtue to do so, and a vice to linger long amid its highways and byways.

Religion has a long history, has been entangled in many cultures, and taken many expressions. Although, at its best, it has challenged cultural assumptions, it has often reinforced them. Our contemporary world is unusual in its rapid technological and other changes. Most times and cultures are slow to adapt and change, so what we now rightly see as great evils (slavery, for example) took many years to end, a long time after some people began to see their malevolence. It is not surprising, then, that religion has been accused of supporting a bigoted and selfish status quo, or patriarchy, or some other social or individual evil.

Quite a few people therefore have a jaundiced attitude towards tradition. This shows itself in a tendency to ignore or even despise religious heritage, or to change it with insufficient thought and care. We can find this today in aspects of Christian worship. Some recent hymnbooks adopt the policy of carrying out such perceived good and necessary works as, for example, removing the masculine pronoun wherever possible from old hymns, and excising any link between God and power and authority. The *Chalice Hymnal* of 1995 (used at the church I attend) effects this and other improvements with great aplomb. In the Preface to this work, its editors claim, enthusiastically:

> With great care and pastoral sensitivity, some hymn texts have been amended to eliminate or reduce archaic language, generic masculine references for humanity, and the negative use of metaphors about darkness or physical disabilities. Language in the hymnal expands the imaging of God in a rich and empowering way.

Well, maybe others should be the judge of the care and sensitivity of this enterprise, and of its overall success. Care and sensitivity are two important qualities, but it is best not to exercise them insouciantly. The hymnbook does not really expand 'the imaging of God in a rich and empowering way'. Instead of (or as well as) making a selective attempt to improve the culture-bound gender assumptions of past hymn writers, the hymnal would have profited from excising some of the more sentimental though popular offerings, and by including more new hymns that attempt to create new images for God that speak to our time and circumstances. An underlying assumption behind this hymnbook appears to be that, if you get the (especially gender) language right, this will result in improved attitudes towards exploited and oppressed people. This may not be so.

When I was a boy, I read Henry Rider Haggard's late-

Victorian adventure story *King Solomon's Mines* with great delight. In some, but by no means all, ways, this book represents stereotypical colonial attitudes towards Africans. Sir Henry Curtis falls in love with an African woman, Foulata, who is killed by the wicked Gagool. Dying, Foulata tells Curtis that their love would not have worked out, for black cannot mate with white. My much younger self was thrilled by this exciting adventure. But it never occurred to me to read out of this story the fact that I could not marry an African woman. No doubt there are some people today who watch James Bond or Indiana Jones or some other adventure movies for tips on how to construct their lives and, as a result, turn to violence or some other deplorable act, but it would be difficult and dangerous to justify banning any artistic venture because some people cannot get the point of what high or low art intends to achieve, or of its culture-bound origins. Moreover, it is more often true that violent and racist people will find justification for their views in (sometimes peculiar interpretations of) books, movies and elsewhere, rather than the point of origin for them.

The *Chalice Hymnal* includes 'My Country, 'Tis of Thee' in its section on 'National Songs' (number 721), and here, very unusually, the editors keep the original words of Samuel Francis Smith, which date to 1831. In a starred endnote, they suggest that the word 'parent' can replace 'father' at two points in the hymn, instead of readily making the changes themselves. I have no way of reading the collective editorial mind that made this decision, but an obvious possibility is that, just as an English hymnbook might hesitate at changing the words to 'God Save the Queen' (both 'songs' use the same tune), a similar tribal taboo exists the other side of the Atlantic Ocean about changing words freighted with the burden of national identity. Yet fervent commitment to the concept of the nation state spilt much twentieth-century blood, and there is something rather distasteful about failing to tackle such a difficult issue. Given the self-congratulatory tone of such ditties, real inclusivism would have wielded a much stronger editorial hand than is the case. The suggested change seems like cheap liberalism.

For a more pointed example, if liturgists and other Christians hold that 'negative views of metaphors about darkness' are grounds for discreet or even flamboyant improvements of texts that use them, what are they to do with the Gospel of John, whose metaphors about darkness, stirring and splendid though they be, can be claimed to have contributed to Christianity's history of anti-Semitism? To change a hymn is one thing. To excise difficult bits of Scripture may be another matter. In the last chapter of this book, we shall consider the importance of worship, what necessary liturgical changes must be done, and how they will be more lasting as well as more authentic if they arise out of a nuanced and respectful attitude towards the faith that has been handed down to us. They also need to go hand in hand with a much more profound analysis of what really needs to change in our culture and the assumptions of Christian worshippers, if we are to live gospel values faithfully and relevantly.

How then are we to find more useful ways, as religious people, of handling our heritage than the well-meaning but ill-considered fumblings of some of our liturgical and other scholars? We could, with profit, turn to some of the human founders of religion for help in this matter.

When I first studied the New Testament in some depth, at the beginning of the 1970s, the influence of German scholarship was all-pervasive. It was impressively learned but, at this distance, it is easy, fun and somewhat necessary to criticize it, for some of its exponents took themselves very seriously indeed. Their work implies that whatever can be known of Jesus is a kind of echo of Hegelian Idealism. Jesus was completely unrelated to his Jewish setting, and is interesting to the scholar and believer only when he appears to have critically distanced himself from his religious background. Some of these scholars wrote of Jesus' milieu as 'late Judaism', as though Judaism died when the Romans destroyed the Jerusalem Temple in

70 CE; troublingly, their words imply that there is, or should be, no such thing as modern Judaism. Given that these scholars lived through the Second World War and Hitler's Holocaust of six million Jews, and that they were still writing of 'late Judaism' when I was a student 30 years later, theirs was a shameful failure of imagination, observation and humanity. A small excuse is that many of them were philosophers trying to ply a historian's trade, without some of the necessary tools for interpreting the evidence convincingly.

In recent years, many scholars have written about the Jewishness of both Jesus and Paul. Ed Sanders has argued that Jesus was, for the most part, a law-abiding Jew. He was indebted to the Hebrew Scriptures, quoting from them and guiding his life by them. He left behind him a group of Jewish and not Gentile followers. Nevertheless, it would be rash to underestimate the radical nature of Jesus' teaching. After all, Christians early on called him Messiah ('Christ' comes from the Greek word for 'Messiah'), and the Gospels claim that that is how the historical Jesus regarded himself, albeit guardedly. That claim in itself would not have rendered him a false teacher in Jewish eyes, though most Jews have never come round to the view that he was the anointed one so, from its earliest days, the Christian movement spread much more widely among Gentiles. Some Jews, however, joined the movement. The community for which Matthew wrote his Gospel included many Jewish Christians, and in it Jesus says that he did not come to abolish the law and the prophets but to fulfil them, and that his disciples' righteousness needs to exceed that of the scribes and Pharisees (5.17–20). This indicates the evangelist's conviction that Jesus was a religious reformer, not a revolutionary. Nevertheless, Jesus did break the commandment to honour one's father and mother: 'Another of his disciples said to him, "Lord, first let me go and bury my father." But Jesus said to him, "Follow me, and let the dead bury their own dead"' (Matthew 8.21–22). Maybe this was a calculatedly shocking statement to a bereaved man. More likely Jesus told him that he should not wait until his father's death before following him; so important is the teaching of the kingdom of heaven that it takes priority over filial piety. Still, however radical and subversive Jesus' teaching was, he stands in the tradition of the prophets of Israel who urged their people to live within God's covenant and challenged them for their failure to do so.

Paul, too, stood foursquare within his Jewish tradition, as Morna Hooker and other scholars have shown. He was not Hellenized to the point of having no links to or understanding of his Jewish heritage. He did not wish to exclude Jews from God's covenant mercies. Rather, he differed from most Jews in believing that Jesus was the Messiah who came to fulfil the Jewish law and incorporate Gentiles as well as Jews within God's promises. Intriguingly, when Paul was arrested and brought before the Jewish council, the author of Acts has him say, 'Brothers, I am a Pharisee, a son of Pharisees' (23.6). His Jewish identity remained important to him, even though he saw himself as the apostle to the Gentiles.

The role of Jesus in the promises of God is an issue upon which the vast majority of Jews and Christians have always disagreed. Even so, neither Jesus nor Paul abandoned their heritage wholesale. They were indebted to the Hebrew Scriptures, and, like many Jews before and since, interpreted the Bible creatively and in ways that some accepted but others did not. They had a creative, admittedly very creative, attitude towards their tradition. But they did not ignore it.

If we look at other human founders of great religious movements, we find similar creative interpretations of the past. The Buddha, the enlightened one, rejected many aspects of Hindu teaching: about caste, for example. Even so, he accepted, though adapted, the basic South Asian worldview of the wheel of samsara from which one struggles to free oneself over the course of many lives. Some Hindus have returned this favour of a creative interpretation of the past, by transforming the

Buddha himself into the ninth incarnation of the Lord Vishnu, following Ram and Krishna. Most contemporary Hindus see this as a positive thing, though some of them realize that Buddhists may not see it that way.

The Muslim Prophet Muhammad condemned the widespread paganism of pre-Islamic Arabia, though there are indications (which have proved controversial among Muslims) that he made overtures (swiftly abandoned) to some of its followers, which would have led them to find a bridge to cross over from their beliefs to submission to the one God. Muslims believe that Muhammad was the revelatory vehicle for their scripture, the Qur'an (meaning 'recitation'). The Qur'an is God's exact words spoken through him, in piecemeal fashion given by the angel Gabriel, over a period of 22 years from 610 until Muhammad's death in 632. It refers 12 times to *hanif* (the plural is *hunafa*). The root meaning of *hanif* is 'to incline' or 'to decline', and a verbal form means 'to turn away from idolatry' or 'to be circumcised'. Eight of the 12 Qur'anic references are to Abraham. Many Muslims use the term to refer to a small number of Arabs before Islam, who believed in one God but were neither Jews nor Christians. They can be said to be proto-Muslims before the coming of Muhammad. There were also Jews and Christians in pre-Islamic Arabia and, at first, Muhammad tried to work with them. The Qur'an makes positive comments about them, particularly Christians. But when most Jews and Christians refused to accept Muhammad as a prophet, he and the Qur'an turned against them. Nevertheless, his followers believed, as do most contemporary Muslims, that Jews and Christians are People of the Book, who received scriptures and are monotheists who believe in Abraham's God – somewhat perversely, Muslims believe, in the case of Trinitarian Christians. Under Sharia law, these scriptured peoples should be treated with tolerance and given *dhimmi* status, as a protected minority, upon payment of a tax.

Here again we find a radical religious leader, who transformed the religious presuppositions of his time. Muhammad criticized much of the religion he found, but did not reject it wholesale. Although many Muslims talk dismissively of the *jahiliyah* (the age of darkness or barbarism) before the coming of Islam, in practice it is clear that Muhammad was much more indebted to his religious heritage than this sweeping generalization permits. And, also in practice rather than through the slogans they sometimes use, Muslims since have sought ways of linking their own religion to God's primordial acts, in ways that affirm God's saving presence in the world ever since its creation.

Indeed, if we are persuaded by the notion that the modern world has somewhat unhelpfully objectified religion into relatively precisely defined religions of choice, then we should not be surprised that those people whom we regard as founders of the great world religions would not have claimed that role for themselves. They would have seen themselves as reformers, sweeping away bad faith in favour of good faith, rather than dumping a bad and boundaried religion so that it can be replaced by a better one. People in the separate ways of faith that eventually emerged would have recognized links with the past, as well as bad things about it that have been (in their view) rightly rejected. It is possible and necessary to question the particular ways in which they resolved issues from their religious past. It is absolutely critical to recognize the importance of that past to them.

There are two extreme and perverse attitudes towards tradition among many contemporary Christians. The first is to accept a particular reading of Christian history and meaning, to the exclusion of much else. The second is to throw the wisdom and the folly of the past overboard, indiscriminately. Take the doctrine of Apostolic Succession, for example. Many Roman Catholics use this to bolster the authority of the Pope as the successor to St Peter as Bishop of Rome. Eastern Orthodox churches agree with Roman Catholics that there has been an unbroken line of bishops since the time of the apostles, but

99

do not grant to the Pope a unique authority. Most Protestants prefer to emphasize the continuity of apostolic teaching. Many Protestants since Martin Luther have also talked of 'the priesthood of all believers', in order, among other things, to reject any idea of a spiritual distinction between the ordained and the laity. Nevertheless, most Protestant denominations and groupings have acknowledged the need for structure and discipline, and accept that some people are called to preside at the Lord's Supper, preach and be a chief pastor to the faithful.

It can hardly be denied that the doctrine of the Apostolic Succession deals with important matters. At stake are such issues as: how do members of the body of Christ access means of grace? How are God's gifts shared for the good of all? How do we distinguish mainstream teaching from false or just insignificant beliefs and practices? Because so many different answers have been given, some of them mutually exclusive and in-your-face competitive, it is easy simply to shout loudly about one of them, and assert it as the clear meaning over against all other bogus ones. Or else it is tempting to condemn the doctrine as out-of-date and utterly meaningless to the contemporary world, and to walk away from it.

These are not the only two ways to proceed, nor are they defensible responses to an important cluster of issues. A better way starts from the observation that any doctrine, however time-honoured, is subject to the investigation of historians and other scholars. University teachers are accustomed to hearing some of their weak students claim that they are entitled to their opinion, when what they really mean is: I am not going to examine any one of my prejudices carefully, in case I am forced to change it; and I deserve an A+ grade anyway, otherwise I am not being valued and neither is my right to choose unthinkingly. Despite the suspicions of many contemporary critics of a religious way of life, many faithful people do not operate like these over-affirmed adolescents. Careful academic work on the Bible and in church history can make significant contributions to the credibility of some doctrinal and other claims to truth. We may not always or even often be able to find the 'right answer' but we can clarify some of the issues that will help us justify the choice or choices we make.

Moreover, it has become increasingly possible to explore divisive theological issues, not as antagonists, but together as people of faith. The greatest achievement of the ecumenical movement has not been its attempts at institutional unity (though some successful outcomes, like the creation of the United Church of Canada in 1925 and of the Church of South India in 1947, were momentous) but its bringing together members of different denominations for serious discussion about difficult issues between them. A Roman Catholic, committed to the primacy of the Pope, most likely is not going to change her mind completely after speaking to a Methodist about ordained ministry. Still, it is possible for the Catholic to have a broader understanding of, for one example, lay participation in the church after such a discussion. And maybe the Methodist would realize that his commitment to the priesthood of all believers did not necessarily entail the laity of all ministers, as he had previously assumed. Perhaps both of them will understand the reasons why differences exist, and respect and even appreciate interpretations that they cannot share. They may also make the deduction that strongly held convictions evolve and adapt over time and in different cultures, so that persons who want them to be always the same thing everywhere, or to make up things afresh for each context, are unlikely to be the official spokespeople for God that some of them aspire to be.

Do not remember the former things?

The great prophet of the exile in Babylon said to his people: 'Do not remember the former things, or consider the things of old. I am about to do a new thing; now it springs forth, do you not perceive it?' (Isaiah 43.18–19). Literalists would take the prophet to be encouraging a collective, communal amnesia. They would also be mistaken.

The prophet was pointing to the return to the land of Israel from exile. This action of God will be greater than any action of the past, even the great exodus under Moses from Egypt to the Promised Land. Isaiah refers to that great prior event to show the greater event to happen. He had sufficient poetry, humour and irony at his disposal to say, in his own way: 'You think that was good? Forget it! Watch this!' But his people would only really understand the gracious future if they knew of God's grace in the past, so that he can always be believed and trusted.

The approach of throwing away or even reinterpreting the past carelessly is to bring about a kind of institutional Alzheimer's disease. The jettisoning of communal memory disables us from learning, reasoning and making right judgements. It is to become a shadow of what we have been and should be. Real Alzheimer's is, of course, a cruel disease, over which people have no choice. For institutions to choose to forget is heedless and reckless stupidity.

That stupidity sometimes arises out of the rampant individualism of our age, and the apparently endless desire of some people for self-affirmation and self-promotion. An individual Christian may feel beyond patriarchy, heterosexism, sectarianism and other unworthy things. So the liberating thing is to start anew, writing on a fresh sheet of paper (to use an analogy from the thought of Chairman Mao, whose ready willingness to start things over made him cheerfully responsible for the death of 70 million people in peacetime). That individual could be faulted on a number of grounds. I mention just four.

Faith is not just about him. He is responsible for other members of the body of Christ. Part of that responsibility involves encouraging others to see his point of view, so that they can change theirs (or, occasionally, even vice versa). Christians who protested and helped bring about, for example, the end of slavery would not have succeeded simply by shouting. They had to persuade and cajole, as well as confront and condemn. Thereby, great causes are won rather than people's little egos affirmed. I found, when teaching in theological college, that this is much more important than being able to say 'I told you so', however pleasing that can sometimes feel, or be necessary to say to some smart-alecs who eventually discover that they do not, after all, know better.

She may also discover friends from the past, to help her in her present endeavours. The patriarchy of the Church has been subverted, in times past, by many woman saints, mystics and religious. Hildegard of Bingen, twelfth-century abbess, musician, and communicator with popes and statesmen; Julian of Norwich, mystic and theologian, whose optimistic belief in a mothering God, even in the plague-ridden fourteenth century, contrasted with most contemporary emphases upon divine judgement; and so on. To 'shake hands with a good friend over the centuries' is to admire what they could do in harder times than our own for a great cause.

We might be tempted, from our supposedly superior vantage point, to suggest that Hildegard and Julian and all the rest of them were all well and good, but what they achieved was seriously constrained by the degrading assumptions of their time. They are therefore of no great help to us. If so, we should consider Jesus' teaching that, with the judgement we make, we will be judged (Matthew 7.1). No doubt, a century or so from now, assuming that we have learned to save our planet by living at peace with it and other inhabitants, some of our spiritual progeny will regard us with withering contempt for the bad things we thought and did that they can clearly see as unworthy ideas and actions. Let us hope that some will spare us the charitable thought that we, too, were bound by false and foolish presuppositions, and that some of us saw beyond them, even if through a glass, darkly; enough to help make their own achievements possible.

If that perception humbles us into taking seriously the achievements of people in other times and places, we might still be tempted to treat the past as though we were spiritually homeless people, looking for good things to sustain us among the garbage of history. Yet we can learn from the totality of the past: about how not to treat people as well as how to affirm them; about how to frame more adequate understandings of God's grace by examining some of the more implausible and even destructive ones. To do this is not to justify acts of darkness, and oppressive beliefs, but to work at their overcoming.

We have already noted L. P. Hartley's observation that 'The past is a foreign country: they do things differently there.' Even so, people of faith believe that God is not without witnesses in every time and place. The past is a mystery, but not an impenetrable one. We need ways of interpreting it for our improving. To these we shall turn in the next chapter.

4

The Heart of Religion

Thou movest us to delight in praising Thee; for Thou hast formed us for Thyself, and our hearts are restless till they find rest in Thee.

The author of these words, St Augustine of Hippo, died in 430, during the siege of that North African city (now Annaba in Algeria) by the Vandals. Although he is one of the fathers of the Western Christian Church, he has proved controversial for, among other things, his views on sin, sex and suffering. Paulos Mar Gregorios, Metropolitan of Delhi and the East in the Malankara Orthodox Church until his death in 1996, once startled an expert on Augustine by saying to him and a group of other Christians from several denominations, 'Augustine is nothing to me.' Later he explained, with a twinkle in his eye, that, from an Eastern Orthodox perspective, Augustine was a provincial bishop of no great importance to the universal Church.

There is rather more to Augustine than that. His *Confessions* (written between 398 and 400, just after he became a bishop) have kindled the imagination of many Christians, both for their honesty and for the confidence they give to those who, like him, have considered and explored many spiritual (and non-spiritual!) options before embracing Christian faith. Augustine came to believe that the heart of religion is a relationship with God. We have been created to be loved by and to love God, and we shall never be completely content and fulfilled until we understand that, and do something about it.

The mainstream Christian belief that God exists, creates us and draws us into fellowship with him is one understanding of religion. There are, of course, alternatives: unconventional Christian takes on religion, as well as many other faith-full or faith-less visions of reality. We have already noted two groups of secular scholars who would deny this core Christian conviction. There are some academics in departments of Religious Studies, many of whom locate their field of work within the social sciences, for whom faith and theology are the red herrings of any study of their discipline. And there are increasingly shrill advocates of neo-atheism, who are convinced that belief in God is irrational and violent, and that that irrationalism and violence is projected by believers onto their false beliefs, making God a bad-tempered monster who reflects and justifies their own absurd ideas and deeds.

As a father has compassion for his children

God: a bad-tempered monster, a creation of distorted human, perfervid imagination? Hostile critics of religion, in arguing that belief in a creator God is unnecessary or even demeaning, ignore, do not know about, or reject Augustine's important point about faith and belief, which he drew from Scripture, that God creates out of love, and seeks the affection of humans rather than their unquestioning obedience.

Not only Jesus but also the psalmist years before him compared God to a father (Psalm 103.13). Normally, children do not attempt to prove the existence of their father. They look for other things from him. While it is natural for many scientists to look for empirical evidence to prove their hypotheses, those among them who think that God is simply an object to be proved or disproved are (to use a phrase with a Qur'anic resonance) in manifest error. Many modern philosophers, at least from Descartes onwards, have handed ammunition to contemporary scholars who assume that God's existence can be disproved on the grounds that science provides the answers for things that used to be thought of as handled by God. If the only reason for God is as the detonator of the big bang, or the architect of the universe, then he can now be viewed as a redundant object. When he is solely the God of the gaps, residing in the presently 'unknown', he is the God of ignorance, and science will more and more illuminate our ignorance, eventually giving God no more places to hide.

Paulos Mar Gregorios wrote of the Enlightenment as a light too bright, keeping humanity from being 'in touch with the Transcendent One, indwelt and enlightened by the One, who alone is the True Light'.[1] Ironically, the powerful torchlight of modernity eclipses all other light. Intending to illuminate the truth, it can blind us to it.

Religious people have known for centuries that it is important to make a case for God's existence, otherwise he is comparable to Father Christmas, the Easter Bunny, the Tooth Fairy, or some other cultural equivalent. But they have made that case not only at the bar of scientific and empirical evidence, but also at other and deeper levels. Some of their attempts to prove God from material data have been more convincing than others. Richard Dawkins scores a few palpable hits, as well as a few cheap ones, in chapter two of his *The God Delusion*, on 'Arguments for God's Existence': he is especially convincing in pointing out the weaknesses of arguments from design. Recent Christian attempts to advocate intelligent design, which seems like a strange hybrid of classical teleological and design arguments for the existence of God, have been amusingly taken to task in Christopher Hitchens' book *God is not Great* but, as so often with his arguments, his case that humans and others are rather badly designed (by evolution, not God), crosses over the line from polemics to frivolousness. When he argues that the design of the universe is not particularly intelligent (humans, for instance, could be much better put together from scratch than how they have actually evolved), he reads like a cultural critic of the day telling Shah Jehan, the seventeenth-century Mughal ruler of North India who caused the awe-inspiring Taj Mahal to be built in memory of his wife, that he, his architects and builders deserve a B– for a good but ultimately imperfect attempt.

Dawkins is able to make his case for God's non-existence because he takes it for granted that judgement is to be delivered entirely in the court of scientific enquiry, and assumes that great thinkers like Aquinas were over-rated duds for arguing outside this artificially imposed arena. This blinkered modernist view has been implicitly accepted, ironically, by many conservative Christians who make a great and nonsensical fuss about literal understandings of Scripture.

For religious people to accept the terms of Dawkins' debate is rather like a meek and innocent man making a foolish and unnuanced attempt to answer the question, 'When did you stop beating your wife?' It is crucial to argue the case for faith in God on other grounds than simply whether he is needed to give a little help to scientific explanations about the world and reality. Most people of faith do not think of God as an object to be proved or disproved but as a way of making sense of and relating to and being transformed by life's deepest meanings.

Christians characteristically call God 'father'. Although Jesus believed God to be creator, he saw him making the deepest impact upon people in being accessible to them in this fatherly way: caring, enduring, hoping and forgiving. The parable of the Prodigal Son, which Helmut Thielicke renamed 'The Waiting Father', focusing the attention upon the God-like figure rather than either one of two spoiled sons, illustrates this powerfully (Luke 10.25–37). This parable has such important things to teach us about God that we must return to it in chapter 5. For the moment, it serves to make the case that, for Jesus, it was not so much God's existence that was at stake, but his relevance and meaning for people. His arguments with some of his Jewish co-believers were not about God's reality but about God's ways in the world.

Jews at the time of Jesus shared the belief that God had called them into a covenant relationship with him. The major covenant had been with Moses on Mount Sinai, as the Jews wandered in the desert before entering the Promised Land flowing with milk and honey. But there had been other covenants before, importantly with Noah and Abraham. This covenant relationship committed God to caring for his people, and them to what has been called, in recent years, ethical monotheism. They were to worship God alone, and treat each other, and strangers within the gate, scrupulously and with justice. God's requirements for Jews were laid out in Torah, his commandments. Important commentators of rabbinic Judaism, which postdates Jesus, located 613 *mitzvot*, or commandments, and that is the view of most Orthodox Jews today. The Jesus movement that sprang up after its founder's crucifixion soon became made up largely of non-Jews. Unlike Judaism and the later related religion of Islam, Christianity abandoned adherence to religious law, though Roman Catholic canon law is part of the same impetus towards enshrining human obligations towards God and the world in carefully considered regulations.

It is clear then that Jews, Christians and also Muslims believe that God enters into a relationship with them, not just as individuals but as peoples of faith. They may bicker about how precisely God reveals himself, and how best to respond to that revelation, but they (and many other people of faith) believe that the transcendent breaks through into the sphere of time and space. God loves persons and peoples. Moreover, although the spiritual children of Abraham recognize that God has it in his power to chastise them for wrongdoing, his overriding desire is to care for and relate to his human creation. The Hebrew Bible talks of God's steadfast love for his people. Jesus spoke of God's fatherly care. When Muslims read their holy scripture, the Qur'an, they notice that every *surah* or chapter except for one begins with an Arabic expression that has often been translated into English as 'In the name of God, the compassionate, the merciful'.

God's steadfast love, fatherly care and mercy are central to monotheistic faith, yet ought not to be sentimentalized. The Hebrew Bible makes it plain that disobedience to God's covenant can lead to catastrophe yet, intriguingly, this never utterly overtakes his people. Disasters do happen to them: notably, the obliteration of the Northern Kingdom in about 722 BCE; the destruction of Solomon's Temple around 586 BCE; and the Babylonian captivity that followed the razing of the Temple. Still, the prophets and other biblical writers believed that God never finally gives up on his people. Moses, according to Deuteronomy, set out the conditions of the covenant to the people in a speech that ends, gravely:

> I call heaven and earth to witness against you today that I have set before you life and death, blessings and curses. Choose life so that you and your descendants may live, loving the Lord your God, obeying him, and holding fast to him; for that means life to you and length of days, so that you may live in the land that the Lord swore to give to your ancestors, to Abraham, to Isaac, and to Jacob. (Deuteronomy 30.19–20)

There were times in Israel's history where such portentous words resonated loudly. The eighth-century BCE prophet Hosea wrote in the shadow of personal and national tragedy. He had married an unfaithful woman, who deserved to be cast off. Hosea draws a parallel between her unfaithfulness and that of his people, who spend their days whoring after other gods than God. His pain and anguish mirror God's:

> How can I give you up, Ephraim?
> How can I hand you over, O Israel? . . .
> My heart recoils within me;
> my compassion grows warm and tender.

I will not execute my fierce anger; . . .
for I am God and no mortal,
the Holy One in your midst,
and I will not come in wrath. (Hosea 11.8–9)

Yet the Northern Kingdom of Israel (sometimes referred to by
the name of one of its tribal groups, Ephraim) was overrun by
the Assyrians soon afterwards, and its people disappeared from
history to re-emerge in mythology as the ten lost tribes of Israel.
The future of the Jews and their faith lay with the Southern
Kingdom of Judah. Hosea's witness was not to a sentimentalized and generalized divine affection. His belief in divine love
was wrung out of his own personal tragedy of loving a woman
and not being loved in return, and seeing in that poignant loss
something of God's anguish over his human children who
cannot be faithful to him or each other.

The prophecy of Hosea gives an intriguing and important
slant on Israel's covenant relationship with God. God's agreement with his people is not best expressed in terms of treaties
between a great king of the ancient world and his vassals,
who are allowed to live only by accepting subservience to him.
Hosea implies that the marriage vow is a better illustration than
a peace treaty of the relationship God covets and expects with
his people. God extends care and love and commitment to
humans.

God is the father or lover or husband of his people. This is the
language of close relationship and, because we have come to
take it for granted, we often fail to see how breathtaking it is to
claim that the mystery that lies within and beyond all things has
a human face (so Christians would say, thinking of Jesus), so
that humans may rest content, enfolded within that loving
mystery. This is not the only way for insiders to depict God: Pat,
to whom God wrote a letter at the beginning of this book's first
chapter, might use the language of love, but in so restrictive a
sense, and so eccentrically, that it does not seem like love to

most people; and non-Christians have different central convictions about transcendent reality (though love is also an important characteristic of the divine for most of them). But Christians above all people of faith, because of the life and teachings of Jesus, and his interpretation of his religious heritage, have to make sense of the concept of God's love for his human children.

God's existence, for most people of faith, is not proved in the laboratory or in mathematical calculations, but by the consequences of his effects in people's lives. If the case for God is to be made in his interaction with his human children, then this raises all sorts of questions about how we can know that this is true.

Religions provide people with a number of ways in which they can find God, or God can find them. We have already noted Baron von Hügel's division of religion into three categories: the institutional; the intellectual; and the mystical. Most religious people are aware of people and places that are set apart to draw attention to and even to mediate God's grace: ministers and churches are examples. Many are aware of the need to offer a reasoned understanding of, and sometimes even a defence for, the faith that is in them: at their best, and sometimes even at their most dreary, sermons do just that as one of their aims. We therefore take for granted the institutional and intellectual dimensions of religion. But what of mysticism?

Although a place for mysticism can be found in Ninian Smart's and Frank Whaling's analyses of the dimensions of religion, it does not stand out there as an important layer of religious experience. Intriguingly, there are many critics of the mystics, or those who play down their importance, and there always have been. Monsignor Ronald Knox, a twentieth-century English crime writer and convert from Anglicanism to Roman Catholicism, observed that mysticism begins in mist and ends in schism. This is an amusing but glib and imprudent comment. Many academics also tout the opinion that mysticism is extraneous to mainstream Judaism, Islam and Christianity; not just irrelevant but dangerous.

In fact, mysticism is central to the Abrahamic faiths, and to most other forms of religious experience. The example of Islam is fascinating and pertinent. It is often portrayed as originally a desert faith, and very austere, so a most unlikely seedbed for mysticism. In reality the seventh-century Arabian peninsular harboured many exotic brands of Christianity, whose adherents were in hiding from the (in their opinion) rigorous, ungenerous and misplaced certainties of post-Chalcedonian Byzantine Christianity. There were unconventional groups of Jews as well; for example, in Yathrib (later called Medina), where Muhammad fled from persecution in 622. There was also paganism in many forms, with poets and seers of whom early Muslims disapproved, though echoes of their elevated kind of speech can be heard in the Qur'an. Islam's supposed austerity is just that: supposed. Also, after Muhammad's death Islam's centre of gravity soon moved away from the desert to urban Damascus, Baghdad and elsewhere. Any contemporary visitor to Islamic lands will know the continuing power of mystical orders, and of dead and living *sheikhs* and *pirs* (friends of God, who knew and know him in powerful ways). The exception is the Arabian peninsular. There, most Muslims have not preserved original and pure Islam; from the eighteenth century onwards, and particularly after the link between the Saudi family and Wahhabi reformers in the twentieth century, they have bought into not so much an austere as a narrow and puritanical interpretation of their religion. They dismiss the mystical dimensions of Islam as superstitious and degenerate. In actual fact, Islamic mysticism or Sufism (properly *tasawwuf*) is Islam's inner dimension and has been called 'the Science of the Heart'. There is a knowledge (knowledge and science derive from the same Latin word) that is known inwardly and by a deep experience of God, not by external analysis of observable data. Words for knowledge in the Bible and the Qur'an imply a profound intimacy: in older English translations of the Bible, it is even used on occasion for sexual intercourse.[2]

Mysticism comes from a Greek word meaning 'to close the eyes'. The mystical experience is not to be had by ordinary experiences or straightforward intellectual effort. It is a transcendent gift, which requires human collaboration to receive and interpret, and the sort of focused concentration that causes someone to screw up or even shut their eyes. So, if religion records the deeds of God who reveals himself to humans and solicits a response to his self-disclosure, then surely mysticism should have a better press than it has in some religious quarters. For it points to and illustrates the human capacity to know and relate to God in profound and intimate ways.

The mystic dimension: communion with God

There are two major strands of religious mysticism. The first is the individual's direct communion or even union with God. The other strand is mystical knowledge: the many, many ways in which knowledge of God independent of the sensory perceptions has been described and lived by mystics.

The first strand can be illustrated by the experiences of religious leaders. Careful attention to stories about Muhammad, the human founder of Islam, reveals a deeply intuitive mystic, who yearned after God. Those stories tell how he would often retire to a cave in Mount Hira, three miles north of Mecca, to pray. On one occasion, when he was about 40 years old, around the year 610, he received a revelation from God, brought by the angel Gabriel (in Arabic, Jibril). Gabriel ordered Muhammad to read out the revelation, and pressed down so tightly upon him with a coverlet of brocade that Muhammad thought he would die. The coverlet had writing on it, which Muhammad recited:

Recite in the name of the Lord who created, created humans from clots of blood. Recite, for your Lord is merciful. He has taught the use of the pen, taught humans what they do not know. (Qur'an 96.1–5)

There was a gap of between six months and three years (Qur'anic commentators vary on this) between this and the following revelation. But Muhammad was thereby set upon and confirmed in his prophetic vocation.[3] A very early revelation describes him as 'enmantled' (74.1), a state of dress that came to be associated with mystics.

The Qur'an (17.1) describes a night journey by Muhammad from the mosque in Mecca to Jerusalem, which has been much elaborated in the Hadith (traditions about the life and sayings of Muhammad). One night when he was in the Ka'bah, a cube-shaped building within the precincts of what is now the great mosque of Mecca, Gabriel awoke Muhammad from sleeping after prayer. He mounted a white beast called Buraq, and sped with the angel to Jerusalem, where they met several prophets, including Abraham, Moses and Jesus. Muhammad acted as prayer-leader for them in the area of the Temple mount. Then he climbed onto Buraq and was taken through seven heavens, accompanied by Gabriel. At each stage, they saw a great prophet: Adam; Jesus; John the Baptist; the Old Testament figure of Joseph; Enoch; Aaron; and Moses. Finally, they saw Abraham. Reflecting later upon this experience, Muhammad is believed to have said: 'I was a prophet when Adam was still between water and clay.' At the summit was a lote-tree. The divine light descended upon the tree and Muhammad gazed upon it, unflinchingly. There he received the command that people should pray 50 times a day but, urged on by Moses, he bartered with God and got him to reduce it to five times. Moses wanted him to ask one more time but Muhammad refused, saying, 'I have returned to my Lord and asked until I am ashamed. I will not go again.' Jewish and Christian hearers of this story would be reminded of the account of Abraham pleading for the people of Sodom, though Muhammad had the more successful outcome: Genesis 18.22–33 records how Abraham got God to agree to save Sodom if ten good people could be found there, but they could not.

This story of Muhammad's night journey to Jerusalem acquired all sorts of meanings for Muslims as it developed over the centuries. It has an element of inter-religious one-upmanship, implying the outstanding status of Muhammad as the last and final prophet of God. Yet it also gives believers a positive sense of their link through other great prophets to previous religious communities. The story's notes of humour and of the fantastic should not be underplayed. Muslims believe the truth or truths of this story. If pressed, many will tell you that they take it literally but, in practice, they play with it, emphasizing this aspect and then another, embellishing it and delighting in it.

It is easy to miss the obvious point that this story is one example of Muhammad the mystic. In occasional moments of exasperation, when speaking with institutionalized imams (mosque functionaries), or with some of the ulema, learned persons who interpret Muslim law, I have been known to suggest, if they frown upon mystical interpretations of Islam, that the prophetic experience itself must surely be a mystical one. Muhammad had, or believed he had, a deep and enduring and special relationship with the Lord of the Worlds.

So, of course, did the prophets of the more distant past. A strong case can be made for the mystical experience of the Hebrew prophets: Moses, Samuel, Elijah and Elisha, among others. By the time of the eighth century BCE, some of the sayings of particular prophets were written down in eponymous scriptural books. These books record God's calling of the prophet to his vocation, which had a common element of recalling recalcitrant people to their covenant relationship with God. When I first studied the Old Testament, my excellent teachers were very keen to point out what the prophets were called by God to do, but we students were never encouraged to reflect deeply on the very unusual fact, to twentieth-century persons, that God spoke to them in the deepest places of their being. In fact, a superficial reading reveals that the prophets' intuitive relationship with God was like a force welling up within them that they could not ignore.

Let us take Jeremiah as an example. He was called as a young man and prophesied to his compatriots for 40 years before the Babylonian exile in 586 BCE and for some time after. Bruised and bloodied by the results of his vocation, he turned in pain and anger to God:

> I have become a laughing-stock all day long;
> Everyone mocks me,
> For whenever I speak, I must cry out,
> I must shout, 'Violence and destruction!'
> For the word of the LORD has become for me
> a reproach and derision all day long.

Although part of him would have liked to have given up his vocation, he could not, as he immediately went on to say:

> If I say, 'I will not mention him,
> or speak any more in his name',
> then within me there is something like a burning fire
> shut up in my bones;
> I am weary with holding it in,
> and I cannot. (Jeremiah 20.7–9)

If mysticism is about a direct communion with God, then this searingly direct language indicates a strong mystical relationship. To read the book of Jeremiah is to encounter a bond between God and his prophet that is intense, angry, bitter, reproachful, honest, and painful. It is also unbreakable, even as the prophet draws close to the edge where faith withers, hope dies and love ends. This is no romantic and sentimentalized relationship. There is a raw honesty in Jeremiah's words that is unforgettable. In any enduring relationship, honesty is a part of the deal, so that, when appropriate (sometimes even when inappropriate), lovers, friends or family members can argue, plead, cajole and give vent to feelings of frustration and anger and hopelessness, when it requires more than one partner thinks he deserves or can give. This is true even of the particular and unique bond between an individual and the transcendent. In the Bible, such honest faith begins at least as early as Abraham, wheedling with God for the people of Sodom. Jeremiah is perhaps the most poignant Old Testament exemplar of this turbulent yet haunting and (for those caught up in it) undeniable relationship between God and his people. Jesus, hanging on the cross and quoting, in agony, Psalm 22.1 ('My God, my God, why have you forsaken me?': Mark 15.34), stands within this tradition of faith.

Written on the Buland Darwaza, the great gateway guarding the north Indian city of Fatehpur Sikri, which was built in 1575 and abandoned soon afterwards, there is an inscription. It is a quote that Muslims attribute to Jesus, and the English translation is: 'The world is but a bridge; pass over but build no houses on it.' Muslims regard Jesus as a great mystic, who distinguished what is important in life from what is trivial and fleeting. Just as Muhammad is the seal of the prophets (Qur'an 33.40), so Jesus is the seal of the saints, according to the Sufi[4] scholar Ibn al-Arabi (d. 1240).

Christians can agree with Muslims about Jesus' status as a mystic, though they want to say that he is more than that. The Gospels' accounts of his baptism indicate the depth of his relationship with God. Characteristically, Mark is short and to the point:

In those days Jesus came from Nazareth of Galilee and was baptized by John in the Jordan. And just as he was coming up out of the water, he saw the heavens torn apart and the Spirit descending like a dove on him. And a voice came from heaven, 'You are my Son, the Beloved; with you I am well pleased.' (Mark 1.9–11)

The evangelist John often depicts the closeness of Jesus' relation to God, to the point where 'the Father and I are one' (10.30). Some New Testament scholars used to argue that this (in their view) higher Christology than that found in the other three Gospels is one strand in an argument for a late dating of the Gospel. The arguments do not seem particularly compelling. After all, Matthew has this passage, the so-called 'bolt from the Johannine blue':

> All things have been handed over to me by my Father; and no one knows the Son except the Father, and no one knows the Father except the Son and anyone to whom the Son chooses to reveal him. (Matthew 11.27)

Moreover, there is some very high Christology expressed or implied in the synoptic Gospels. For example, if Jesus' calling of 12 disciples indicates the gathering into God's kingdom of the 12 tribes of Israel, than what manner of person is it who sets himself outside, not within, these tribes as their master? I owe this observation to my Cambridge New Testament teacher, C. F. D Moule, who also argued that such passages indicate that the Christology of the fourth and fifth centuries, enshrined in the creeds, was a development from the teaching of the earliest witnesses to Jesus; it was not an innovation. Whatever may be the case, early Christians certainly believed that Jesus shared a close and intimate association with God. Most Christians then and now have regarded it as uniquely close. Even so, Jesus drew his disciples into the ambit of that relationship: 'He said to them, "When you pray, say: Father, may your name be held holy . . ."' (Luke 11.2).[5] This is an intriguing juxtaposition of imagery. The word 'Father' signifies a close relationship, whereas holiness has a range of meanings, including 'set apart' from the normal and the usual. Jesus' disciples are encouraged to recognize that they have an intimate relationship with the high and lofty one who inhabits eternity.[6] God loves, yet remains God, the beyond in our midst, never to be taken for granted.

Persons who are deeply attached to the notion that the scientific method alone can unravel the skein of truth may find any claim to mystical experience unsettling, even bizarre, and are sure to misunderstand it. Even some believers with a prosaic turn of mind get the wrong impression of what the mystics intend. Mystics use heightened language to describe things that are too deep for everyday language. When Jesus described the bond between the Father and the Son, he need not necessarily have been in contravention of the Shema: 'Hear, O Israel: The LORD is our God, the LORD alone' (Deuteronomy 6.4). At the very least, however, he or his earliest followers pulled Jewish monotheism just about as far as it will stretch. Precisely because mystical language is heightened, there is an element of imprecision that enables others to argue and debate what mystics or their followers intended to convey. We shall offer some examples later in this chapter.

The mystical dimension: mystic knowledge

Mystics believe that they meet God in the depth of their being. They seek the knowledge and love of God and, in encountering this, find their lives transformed. The best way of illustrating this is through examining the lives of some such people. But before we embark upon this enterprise, we should note one important thing.

Although the mystical experience is powerfully illustrated in the lives of some people, religious founders and saints among them, it is different only in degree and not in kind from an experience that is open to all who have faith and hope and love. In almost every church and chapel, synagogue and temple and mosque, there are people whose lives are lit up by the joy of God's presence. They do not usually describe themselves as mystics, though the basis of their experience is the same as that of, say, the prophets of old. They have not been called to the same vocation, rather to faithfulness in their own generation and circumstances, but they have felt God's touch upon their lives, in some way or other. If they are Christians, then, in worship and in the reading of Scripture, they discover the knowledge and conviction that God is father (and, as we shall see, mother, among many other images).

When I went through the process of becoming a Methodist minister, I was troubled and irritated though also amused by the number of times I had to give an account of my experience of God. I wondered why church meetings had such a need to hear of another's spiritual story; was it, perhaps, that their own experience was somewhat tired and stale? I also had the strong (maybe cynical) impression that some candidates were milking the details of their spiritual life for all they were worth and a bit more; and I was not above playing to the gallery myself. Still, something important lay behind this ritual, even if it was capable of being abused. The important thing was not that the clergy (and future clergy) should be able to impress the laity by their greater spirituality, but that all Christians should be able to locate moments that are filled with divine splendour. The trouble is that humans are often impressed by the extraordinary instead of what George Herbert called 'Heaven in ordinarie'. Few people receive a call as powerful and obvious as that of, say, Samuel (1 Samuel 3.1–18). But many can attest to a moment or moments when God has spoken effectively and profoundly to them in the ordinary stuff of life: maybe, for example, when they have cradled their firstborn in their arms and realized that a strictly scientific account of what they are experiencing does not do complete justice to it.

It is appropriate to begin our examples of the mystics with an act of filial piety, and introduce John Wesley. At first blush, he appears an eccentric choice. He offends many instinctive notions of what mystics should be. He was, after all, a busy man, spending many years travelling Britain and Ireland to preach and teach, to set up local societies, and to make sure they were adequately supervised when he was not there to keep a personal eye on proceedings. He was sometimes bad at close personal relations and a bit of a control freak. If the measure of a mystic is solitude, freedom from the world's obligations, and a touch of holiness, then maybe John is not your man. Still, consider what people still call his conversion experience of 24 May 1738 in Aldersgate Street, London:

> About a quarter before nine, while he [the reader] was describing the change which God works in the heart through faith in Christ, I felt my heart strangely warmed. I felt I did trust in Christ, Christ alone for salvation; and an assurance was given me that he had taken away my sins, even mine, and saved me from the law of sin and death.

The religious life is made up of many conversions, turning from one point of view to another, or deepening it by embracing other perspectives. It makes sense to think of this as that kind of conversion experience, but no sense at all to regard it as the definitive moment when Wesley became a 'real' or a 'sound' Christian. That is a trivial reading of his life, and of this experience as one, albeit very important, stage in it. John's reading of William Law in the mid 1720s, and his reading of the church fathers, especially the fathers of the Eastern Church and their emphasis upon *theiosis* (the doctrine that persons can become, by grace, divinized, as Jesus was by right), were at least as important indicators of his mettle as a Christian as was the

Aldersgate experience. Moreover, in June 1766 he wrote to his brother:

> I was saying I do not feel the wrath of God abiding on me; nor can I believe it does. And yet (this is the mystery) [I do not love God. I never did.] Therefore [I never] believed in the Christian sense of the word. Therefore [I am only an] honest heathen, a proselyte of the Temple, one of the God-fearers.

This rather endearing self-doubt suggests that it is foolish to place Wesley's spiritual life in pigeon-holes marked before and after 1738.

Regard the Aldersgate event as a mystical experience, however, and it makes much better sense than as an overwhelming conversion experience. Mystical moments often arise out of the, if not quite commonplace and mundane, rather unspectacular. In Wesley's case, he went to a Moravian meeting, and heard someone read the preface to Luther's commentary on Paul's epistle to the Romans. The words touched something deep within him, confirmed the relationship with God that he had long struggled with, and made sense of all he had done and been. They set his vocation on a particular track, of which Methodism is one result.

The difference between a merely ascetic way of life and a mystical one is the gift of love, which lies at the heart of a close encounter between the divine and the human. It was surely Wesley's mystical relationship with God that made him strive after 'perfect love' or 'entire sanctification'. He had been interested in holiness since his readings of Law and others, and participated in his brother Charles' Holy Club in Oxford from 1729 until he went to Georgia in 1735. Perhaps John's Aldersgate experience made him less priggish and Pelagian about holiness: less inclined, in other words, to think that the hard work of prayer and good deeds could improve a person; and more aware of resting in a gracious relationship that gave prayer and good deeds joy and meaning. In his *Plain Account of Christian Perfection* (1767), he describes holiness as a state of the soul, desiring to be 'perfect as the father in heaven is perfect'. His teaching on sanctification has long been controversial, since it seems to imply that, in this life, people can become perfect. This connotation is no more notorious than the words of Jesus in Matthew 5.48: 'Be perfect, therefore, as your heavenly Father is perfect.' No doubt Wesley was indebted not just to Scripture but also to his reading of the Eastern fathers' teaching about *theiosis*. It is possible, indeed likely, that he overplayed his hand in his teaching about holiness, given his temperament and talents. Still, like Jesus, he believed that others can be drawn into a close and life-changing relationship with a good God. And, in the heightened language of divine–human encounter, there are perfect moments that give meaning to and hope for the imperfect ones. They encourage Christians to believe, even to be utterly persuaded, that what is momentarily experienced is a glimpse and foreshadowing of the joys of the life of heaven.

Compare John Wesley's Aldersgate experience with the apostle Paul's, and it is clear that both are in the same sphere of divine–human encounter. Paul was another force of nature, travelling far and wide to set up communities of faithful people and eager to keep them on the straight and narrow when he was away from them. Christians have reason to be grateful for this, since it produced his letters, alternately cajoling and condemning, congratulating and inspiring his readers (and hearers, since presumably his letters would have been read aloud to many more than those who read them). Many Christians celebrate the feast of the conversion of St Paul on 25 January each year. Here again, the question arises as to whether conversion is the correct word. He was not converted from Judaism to Christianity, for the two religions were not completely separate entities during his lifetime. Paul regarded himself as a Jew who believed that Jesus was the Messiah through whom God drew the Gentiles into his covenant relationship. Acts 23.6 has Paul say to members of the Jewish council: 'Brothers, I am a Pharisee, a son of Pharisees.' Admittedly, this was part of a carefully crafted speech to divide the assembly into those who believed in the resurrection of the dead (the Pharisees) and those who did not (the Sadducees), but there is no reason to believe that Paul was simply playing the role of cynical manipulator. His own letters, as well as the book of Acts, make it plain that Paul saw himself as a Jew, albeit an eccentric and marginal one from the perspective of most of his co-religionists, then and now.

Paul's Damascus Road experience did not transfer him from one religion to another. It drew him into a relationship with God through an encounter with the risen Lord Jesus: this Christ-mysticism was to be a lifelong inspiration to him thereafter: 'I have been crucified with Christ; and it is no longer I who live, but it is Christ who lives in me' (Galatians 2.19–20). One on occasion, and reluctantly, he described his mystical experiences, at one remove from them, as though such encounters were too wonderful and private to speak of lightly:

> I know a person in Christ who fourteen years ago was caught up to the third heaven – whether in the body or out of the body I do not know; God knows. And I know that such a person – whether in the body or out of the body I do not know; God knows – was caught up into Paradise and heard things that are not to be told, that no mortal is permitted to repeat. (2 Corinthians 12.2–4)

Paul has had something of a bad press in modern times. He is regarded by many as a misogynist, even though many of his associates were women. Rumour also has it that he turned the simple message of Jesus into complicated doctrine that created the Christian Church and has misdirected it ever since. The author of 2 Peter, though not the brightest star in the New Testament firmament, had a point when he wrote of 'our beloved brother Paul' that 'there are some things in them [Paul's letters] hard to understand' (3.15–16). Still, Paul's is a mind that it is a privilege to grapple with, wrestling as he did at depth with such a tremendous experience of God's transforming friendship.

When we read the Pastoral Epistles (1 and 2 Timothy, and Titus) which, though put out in Paul's name, come from a generation later, it is possible to feel both relief and dismay: relief, because the letters are much easier to understand than the authentic epistles; dismay because, theologically and experientially, nothing of any comparable standard to Paul's theology is being imparted. It is an exaggeration to say that we have moved from mission to maintenance, but a pardonable one. The Pastoral Epistles have provided later generations of church historians, theologians and liturgists with the raw material for constructing doctrines about the Church, including ordained ministry; useful and necessary, but humdrum and lacking Paul's genius. By the end of the first century of the Common Era, the Church was becoming institutionalized. This was necessary, in order for the message of Jesus to be handed down from generation to generation. But it came at a cost: to move from the meaning of justification to the purpose of presbyters has its intellectual drawbacks, and can encourage bishops, clergy and other beneficiaries of organized religion to think themselves and what they stand for to be far more important than is the case.

Still, Paul himself founded a number of churches in the eastern Mediterranean region and, after he realized that Jesus would not come again in his lifetime, no doubt wanted them to survive him. His own theology is for the Church: it is not simply individualistic but communal. He described Christians as members of the body of Christ, working together for the common good, empowered by the Spirit to do so; and the greatest gift of the Spirit is love. That love is not self-love but love for all, because Christ died for all. Paul would have agreed with John Wesley that 'Christianity is essentially a social religion; and that to turn it into a solitary one is to destroy it'.[7]

The social dimension of Christianity does, however, arise out of an intensely individual experience. Getting the balance right in the contemporary world is difficult. There are many people who sincerely seek to follow Jesus but who have been alienated by the institutional churches. Although clergy can be figures of Christ-like love, they can also defend values that privilege themselves and exclude others; as, indeed, can some of the laity, especially ones who are busy working at curtailing what they see as wrongful ministerial privileges so that they can shore up their own. Moreover, it is sometimes hard to live in community with other Christians. I well remember one usually charitable person describing a man unknown to me as an armpit in the body of Christ. Yet Wesley's condemnation of the solitary Christian also has a point: if love is at the heart of the mystical divine–human encounter, then it is appropriately shared with others, however tiresome and unattractive they may be. Else it may, and often does, turn inwards in egoism instead of outwards in compassion.

Some mystics, however, shun religious institutions. This is not because they are self-centred spiritual athletes, determined to win the race at whatever cost to themselves and others. It is mostly because their experiences and their temperaments make them more aware of the sinful actions of religious institutions than their capacity for good. One of the most intriguing of twentieth-century mystics was Simone Weil, born to an agnostic Jewish family. She became deeply attracted to aspects of the Roman Catholic Church, but never formally converted. Her high standards meant that she felt unworthy to be a Christian; she was also unwilling to join a church that exhibited all too human frailties. She was nevertheless profoundly affected by three encounters with Catholic life. The first was the celebration of a saint's day in a Portuguese village; the second was a time of prayer in St Francis' Assisi; the last and most overwhelming was the Easter week liturgy at Solesmes Abbey, where the chanting of the monks transported her. She felt that the Passion of Christ suffused her being. She had many mystical experiences. Having been introduced to George Herbert's poem 'Love', she learned it by heart and, on an occasion when she was reciting it, she felt that, as she later laconically wrote, 'Christ came down and took me.' This was one of a number of such occasions. She later experienced him in a way 'infinitely more real, more moving, more clear than on that first occasion when he took possession of me'. Weil was also profoundly affected by philosophy, eastern as well as western: she learned Sanskrit so as to be able to read the *Bhagavad Gita* in the original. She wrote widely on affliction. In 1942, she escaped France for England with her parents. Although ill, she refused to take food out of solidarity with her French compatriots suffering under the Nazi jackboot. As a result, she died at the early age of 34.

Was Weil deranged? Her slow act of suicide, for such in practice it was, does not seem on the surface to be the action of a totally integrated person. It is possible to look at many celebrated mystics (such as Joan of Arc or John of the Cross) and to explain their experiences (or some of their experiences) as the result of mental illness. Since there are many equally celebrated mystics who are outwardly well-adjusted people and responsible citizens, it will not do to claim that mysticism can always be put down to lunacy, sexual repression, or some other perceived human weakness, though sometimes this has doubtless been the case. Mystics are not perfect people. Some of them may be particularly frail and fragile, yet glow with the divine light. Mystics are individuals who try to make sense of a world that, for all its imperfections, they know to be created out of transcendent love and goodness. Those who come close to the fire of love and are warmed by it may not act in ways that seem sensible to others whose experience is not so heightened. And there are some mystics who are seared, almost burned up, by the consuming flames of God's presence, among them Francis with the stigmata, the wounds of Christ's Passion, on his hands and feet, and Simone Weil, identifying with the world of pain and suffering and so embracing the ecstasy of God's eternal presence.

Weil's identification with French people suffering under German occupation, not least other Jews who were rounded up and taken to death camps, is an example of the mystics' involvement with the suffering and wounded world. The mystical experience, though deeply personal, identifies with God's love for the world. Many people, for whom action comes more easily than meditation, are puzzled by the actions of Weil and others who live in and interpret the world differently than they do. In the 1960s and 1970s, and even in our own time, some Christians condemned the monastic vocation, particularly enclosed orders, as self-indulgent and pointless. Yet, if one believes in the power of prayer, such condemnation is unwise. Especially if prayer is interpreted, not as a wish list to be ticked off as God grants each request, but as a deep relationship with God, to whom one can offer the hopes and needs of the world, in love, and in the faith and hope that all will be well, because of God's grace.

Mother Julian of Norwich coined the expression, 'All shall be well, and all shall be well, and all manner of thing shall be well.' In May 1373, ill and at the point of death, she was gifted with a series of 16 visions, and recovered. She wrote a book about her experience called *Showings*. We have it in two editions. The first was probably penned shortly after her visions, whereas the second was written after many years' reflection upon them. One of the most famous and touching of her illustrations concerns seeing something small, no bigger than a hazelnut, in her hand, and realizing that this represented everything God has made. She was assured that it lasts, as it always will, because of God's love. The Black Death had killed up to two-thirds of Europe's population when it spread there in the late 1340s. At that time, Julian was a small child. Yet this could not dampen her sense of God's love. She saw that suffering was not a punishment from God; in her case, it had been a blessing, drawing her close to God. All can and must be seen in the context of God's love.

Although she lived life after her illness as an anchoress attached to a church in Norwich, in prayer and contemplation, many people came to see her. They were entranced by her fame as a spiritual woman, but also by the quality of her writing and its witness to her fervent faith.

Mother Julian's attitude towards suffering puzzles many people, for whom the world's suffering is the greatest obstacle to believing in the goodness of God. The problem of suffering has vexed all of the world's religions and ideologies, and there is no clear-cut answer to it. Christian mystics, not just Julian but many others, have seen and interpreted it in the context of a relationship with God that seems so real that not even suffering (or, as we shall see in the final chapter, death) can destroy it. Because Jesus himself was not spared suffering, many mystics have been willing, even glad, to share in his sufferings in order thereby to be, as they see it, a witness to it as a source of healing for others.

The mystical dimension: aims and goals

It is quite easy to describe the aim and goal of a mystic: to experience the love of God, to share that love so that others will truly know it, and ultimately to be united with God. But the experience can be so intense, and our human language is so inadequate to describe it, that a bald summary can be misleading.

Over time, the mystic path has been divided by Christian mystics and scholars into three stages through which mystics pass before the ultimate goal of union with God. It is a *scala perfectionis*, a ladder of perfection, beginning, on the lower rungs, with the purgative life. Mystics practise detachment, renunciation and asceticism, turning from the sensory world and from self to God's unchanging reality. This leads to the contemplative life, in which the mystic lovingly contemplates God, rejoicing in the mystery of God and of all that exists. Finally, there is the illuminative life, living in union with God, a relationship of radiant ecstasy. This unity is sometimes described in Jesus-language and sometimes in God-language: one can be said, for example, to be united with Jesus or lost in God. Some mystics use both ranges of images.

The vast majority of Christian mystics stop short of claiming identity with God, who remains other, the creator not the created. But some mystics, including Meister Eckhart, who died in 1327, have used language that is capable of being understood as unity in the oneness of all being. He got into trouble with ecclesiastical authorities because of this. Four centuries earlier, the Muslim Persian Sufi mystic Mansur al-Hallaj had been in even more trouble with the religious and political establishment of his day; indeed, they executed him in March 922, probably by crucifixion or perhaps by beheading. One of the reasons for this severe verdict was that he was known to claim, ecstatically, '*Ana al-Haqq*,' 'I am truth'; *haqq*, or truth, is one of the Muslim names of God. Was Hallaj claiming absolute identity with God? He may have been, but probably not. In rare ecstatic moments, the uncreated divine Spirit can merge with the created human spirit, like the sun obliterating the moon momentarily in an eclipse. Then, such words as Hallaj's can signify that fleeting ecstasy.

Muslim mystics, like Christians, believe that love lies at the heart of the divine–human encounter. They make a great deal of the Qur'anic account of God's primordial covenant with humankind, recorded in Q7.171. God called forth future humanity from the loins of Adam, before he created him, and solemnly spoke to them the words: 'Am I not your Lord?' They replied, 'Yes, we witness it.' The mystics' goal is to return to the day of that primordial covenant, when God alone existed, before he created humans and endowed them with life, love and understanding so that they might return to him on the Day of Judgement.

The rich history of Islamic mysticism produced even more elaborate methodologies for understanding Sufism than Christians created in order to interpret their own mystical experiences. Corresponding to the Christian division of the purgative, contemplative and illuminative life is the Islamic definition of *sharia*, *tariqa*, and *haqiqa*. The *sharia* is Islam's holy law. Mystics do not bypass its demands, but see the mystic path as a branch leading out of the divine highway that is God's law. The *tariqa* is the 'path' that leads the devotee through different stages until she or he slowly reaches the goal of *tauhid*, knowing fully the unity of God. That is *haqiqa*, the 'truth'. The penultimate stage is *fana* ('extinction' or 'passing away'), when the individual's shortcomings and mundane ties are annihilated and she or he is absorbed into God. In this stage, a person does not lose individuality but dies to himself or herself so as to be born in God. In the final stage of *baqa* ('abiding'), the individual rests or abides or subsists in God.

There are differences between Christian and Muslim mystical experiences, and not just the obvious one of the importance of Jesus to the former and the greater significance of Muhammad to the latter. Muslim Sufis are far more likely to seek the guidance of a *sheikh* or 'spiritual guide' than are Christian mystics. Indeed, a saying exists in Islam that 'when someone has no *sheikh*, Satan becomes his *sheikh*'. The master guides the disciple's spiritual growth. This is similar to many Hindu convictions about the individual's need for guidance from a human who has walked the mystic path for far longer than she or he has. From about the twelfth century CE, many Sufi orders were established, under the guidance of a *sheikh*, and they still flourish in many parts of the Muslim world.

These steps on the mystics' journey obviously point to something important. Put simply, the bond that a mystic has with God needs to be developed and sustained in order for her or him to achieve the goal of unity with the divine. No human relationships can endure on the basis of a moment's joyfulness, however ecstatic. The same is true of an individual's experience with the divine. Occasionally, one gets the impression from writers on mysticism that the useful device of various stages, steps and ways has become freighted with more meaning than it can bear. It is like listening to some solemn theologian describe, with far too much information and detail, what he (or she; though it more often is he, in my experience) means by the doctrine of the Trinity, and reaching that moment where you wonder if he has ever heard of metaphor or read any poetry. So far as I am aware, John Wesley did not apply the findings of the mystical theoreticians to his own Aldersgate and other private experiences. Even so, such things as his doctrine of holiness and his life of prayer illustrate what those methodologies point to: the consequences and goal of a close and deepening relationship with God.

The mystical dimension: a gift to the Church

The mystical experience is only one of the many dimensions of being Christian. It does need careful attention, however, because many Christians are needlessly suspicious of it, or else regard it as irrelevant to their own faith. Yet it illustrates, to a high and in a heightened degree, 'knowledge' that should be common to all people of faith: the divine desire to love humans, and the human capacity to know and respond to this.

There are some ways in which the mystics' experiences challenge common assumptions about Christian life and faith. For many Christians, the heart of Christian faith is the institutional Church. Even for many who claim otherwise, it is. Members of house-churches or other congregations who set their faces against the evils of denominationalism mostly privilege the institutionalization of religion. The many non-denominational churches in the USA, often founded to air someone's eccentric views or to house the Spirit who (it is often assumed) has turned her back on mainstream churches, are thoroughly institutionalized. Most substitutes for churches end up with leaders, particular ways of worshipping God, and a set of convictions you need to believe in order to belong. At their worst, their 'members' have not read Jesus' parable of the Pharisee and Publican (or tax collector) carefully enough (Luke 18.9–14) and so are very ready to thank God that they are not as other people. Ironically, they are.

For all the faults of churches, whether distinct denominations or specific worshipping communities, at their best they keep alive the story of Jesus, provide homes for the human spirit and encourage people to live caringly for others. Yet the human habitual preference for hierarchy, social stratification and other bureaucratic things, sometimes more necessary than its critics maintain, can nevertheless hinder the effects of the divine Spirit. So can the besetting propensity for humans to justify convenient convictions by reading their preferences into Scripture or projecting them onto God.

Mysticism wonderfully subverts institutional priorities. For example, as we look back at the history of the medieval Church, few but professional historians will have heard of the great popes of that period though many will know the stories of St Francis. He walked with God, talked amicably with a sultan in North Africa at a time when crusades had blighted Christian relations with Muslims, and his creation theology may be coming into its own in our environmentally conscious age. In 1209, he received permission from Pope Innocent III to found a new religious order. Innocent was Pope from 1198 to 1216, and an energetic upholder of papal power, bullying rulers, calling for a crusade, and summoning a council that required Jews and Muslims to wear distinctive clothing. From our perspective, Francis seems the more memorable figure, as well as the more Christ-like one. Holy Christians are a constant source of inspiration to us when we meet or read of them. But it is unwise of Christians in any denomination to look to its bureaucrats for all (occasionally even for some) of the gifts of the Spirit that make the Church a place of hope and holiness. Often they create or at least favour doctrines and practices that entrench their position rather than encouraging the Spirit to blow where she will.

The vast majority of such Christians have been men, so it is not surprising that Christianity has, like most religions, been patriarchal. The first woman to be ordained to any church was Antoinette Brown Blackwell, who was called to be pastor of the South Butler Congregational Church in New York in 1853. Even so, the denomination did not recognize her ordination and she left it in 1854 to become a Unitarian. The Roman Catholic and Orthodox Churches, as well as many Protestant Churches, still refuse to ordain women. However, from earliest times, many Christian mystics have been women.

At a time when women's roles in Christianity were even more circumscribed than now, some women exercised influence because they were seen as Spirit-filled. We have already mentioned Julian of Norwich. Her writings make a great deal of the motherhood of God. She described Christ memorably as 'our mother, brother and saviour', and elsewhere widely extended the repertoire of familial images that bind together God and his human children: 'God rejoices that he is our Father, and God rejoices that he is our Mother, and God rejoices that he is our true spouse, and that our soul is his beloved wife.' Some contemporary liturgists (editors of hymnbooks, for example) could learn from Julian about using a greater range of images for God instead of employing commonplace grammatical devices (like substituting the plural for the masculine singular), and from her ability to choose intriguing but appropriate new or unusual images, rather than unhelpful and misleading ones (such as replacing 'father' with 'creator', about which more later).

Another extraordinary woman mystic lived 200 years before Julian, and in the German Rhineland. Hildegard of Bingen was the abbess of a convent, a musician and composer, a painter, a writer about medicine, a traveller and a preacher. She produced a trilogy of spiritual books, which she dictated to her scribe, a monk. She wrote to male church leaders, including the Pope, and was not above giving them good advice. As she lay dying on 17 September 1179, it is recorded that two streams of light appeared in the sky and formed a cross. She had taught that God was *lux vivens*, the 'living light', and her inclusive visions emphasized that God's work on earth needs to be carried out by men and women together.

It would be trivial and impertinent to suggest that the experiences of women mystics like Hildegard and Julian help offset, still less justify, centuries of patriarchal practice. Many women must have suffered greatly for their brave and stressful commitment to following the dictates of their conscience and the voice of their experience with the divine. Hildegard, for example, was often ill with what could have been migraines, a result of tension in her life and vocation. Yet they do enable us to hear other voices above the din of male ones. And such women mystics seem remarkably relevant to our own day, with our need to relate God's love to a diverse and plural world.

One of the issues of our plural world is how we are to relate to people of other religions. There are plenty of examples of appalling inter-religious relations in the world, in which Christians (but not just Christians, as some people oddly and foolishly claim) are often involved as a guilty party. Christian anti-Semitism has with some justification been called 'the longest hatred'. Islamophobia stalks the contemporary world, causing Christians, Jews and secularists to lump together terrorists and saints in a single violent interpretation of Islam. The next chapter will deal at more length with Christian understandings of truth in a diverse world. But it is important and relevant here to underline what we have already illustrated: that the mystical experience is a universal one that no more privileges Christians than it does males. One of the most widely read mystical writers in the West is the thirteenth-century Central Asian Muslim, Jamal al-Din Rumi, who spent many years in Konya, Turkey, and is buried there. Although he was himself a scholar of Muslim religious law, he despised those who saw the law as an end in itself and used their knowledge of it to cultivate their self-importance: he described them as 'curs, baying at the moon'. The *mevleviyya* Sufi order of whirling dervishes claims spiritual descent from him and, according to one interpretation, their dance attempts to emulate the motion of the spheres. These words are associated with him, and many Muslims, especially Turks, will spontaneously and joyfully recite them when encouraged to do so (and sometimes when not):

> Return (in repentance), return! Whatever you are, return! Even if you are an unbeliever or a Magian[8] or an idol worshipper, return! This court of ours is not a court of despair. Even if you have broken your repentance a hundred times, return!

These are not the words of an Osama or a Pat. Here is the evocative and universal language of divine love that Mr Wesley would have recognized, even if he would have had strong things to say about the need for holiness as a response to such grace.

A widespread mistake among some Christian practitioners of interfaith dialogue is to underplay or even trade in important beliefs, such as Trinitarian or Christological doctrines, in a misguided search for some common ground. The experience and practice of Christian mystics would argue against that: many described their union with God in strongly Christological language; and many also described the Trinity in relational terms, seeing in the image of the Father's relation to the Son and the Spirit a way of identifying the closeness and complexity of their own relationship to God. At the same time, the mystics' acceptance of orthodox doctrine was in the context of their understanding of all religious language as pointing to truths that are beyond the capacity of language adequately to describe. Religious language is heightened language, just as the mystical experience is heightened experience.

Would that more theologians saw the implications of this truth! St Augustine wrote: 'God is not what you imagine or think you understand. If you understand him you have failed.' If systematic theologians sometimes give the impression of wanting to understand God, down to the last detail, mystics have more characteristically wanted to bathe in the divine ocean of being. This implies rather different views about truth. To this issue of truth, we must now turn.

5

The Power of the Truth

As a child, I loved the hymn 'When a knight won his spurs in the stories of old'. I still do. Those of a literalist cast of mind would no doubt think that I should, by my advanced age, have given up childish things; things which, moreover, invite a superficial response of pursed lips and tapping fingers. For, on a surface reading, this hymn is full of deplorable militaristic and violent images, is patriarchal through and through (though written by a woman, Joyce Placzek, under the pseudonym of Jan Struther), and imposes an adult's outlook on the world while condescendingly presenting a child's viewpoint. The hymn's third and last verse runs:

Let faith be my shield and let joy be my steed
'Gainst the dragons of anger, the ogres of greed;
And let me set free, with the sword of my youth,
From the castle of darkness, the pow'r of the truth.

Maybe it is better read as childlike rather than childish. When Jesus said of little children that 'it is to such as these that the kingdom of God belongs' (Mark 19.14), presumably he was encouraging adult disciples to be childlike. Children are open to wonder; see meanings within meanings; grapple with an imaginative view of the world to deal with concepts like faith, joy, anger, greed, freedom, darkness and truth; and are often unnervingly able to get to the heart of the matter when adults shield themselves from it by imposing layers of excuses that pass for meanings or by passing judgements on things that might otherwise catch them unawares and change them for the better.

Children, however bright and wise beyond their years, also have to grow into knowledge and understanding, whereas many atrophied adults (as I discovered when Academic Dean in a theological college) think that they have already passed that test. One of the hymn's achievements is to appeal to the Arthurian legends, popular in its day, to present a relationship with God as an adventure or a journey, like the knight's quest for the Holy Grail, or even to rescue a princess from a dragon.

The 'pow'r of the truth' comes at the end of a quest, is to be found on a journey. The mystics know this to be so, as we have discovered, not just for spiritual athletes like themselves but for all people of faith. We have to pass through various stages of self-discovery, and of encounters with the divine, before we reach its goal.

John Wesley's younger brother Charles was as much of a mystic as he. Perhaps his most beloved hymn describes this goal in its final verse:

> Finish, then, thy new creation;
> pure and spotless let us be.
> Let us see thy great salvation
> perfectly restored in thee;
> changed from glory into glory,
> till in heaven we take our place,
> till we cast our crowns before thee,
> lost in wonder, love, and praise.

Wrestling Jacob

The early Methodists learned their understanding of God as they sang their hymns. They were fortunate to have the talents of Charles Wesley and of his much older contemporary non-conformist Isaac Watts (who died in 1748) at their disposal. The great Congregationalist scholar Bernard Manning, in a lecture of 1937, claimed that Watts had the greater mind but that Wesley was the greater artist. He also observed that together 'they form a heritage that only a madman will let slip'. Words of prophecy, indeed, for though Watts and Wesley occasionally faltered, they stopped well short of some contemporary efforts to trivialize the faith handed down to us. If Methodism was born in song, it is now dying (or at least deluged) in doggerel.

'Love Divine, all loves excelling' may be Charles' best-known hymn, but his finest was 'Wrestling Jacob'. Isaac Watts said, with pardonable exaggeration, that 'Come, O thou traveller unknown' was worth all that he himself had ever written. After Charles died, John broke down on an occasion when he was teaching the hymn to a group of people, a measure not just of his affection for his brother but of the power of his words.

The hymn is about Jacob wrestling with God, recorded in Genesis 32.22–32. Many Christian mystics have favoured stories about Jacob: the tale of Jacob's dream of a ladder descending from heaven (Genesis 28.10–22) is often used by them to describe the rungs of mystical experiences leading to God. Yet Jacob was a shady character, stealing his older brother's blessing and inheritance. He is one of the Bible's great tricksters, a conman. Even in the story of his wrestling with God, he gives the impression of wanting to know his opponent's name for no better reason than to have power and advantage over him. Still, when he knew that he had 'striven with God and with humans, and . . . prevailed', he called the place Peniel, 'the face of God', and was overwhelmed by the experience of having seen God and lived to tell the tale. He was indeed fortunate. Both Old and New Testaments of the Christian Bible make plain the infinite, qualitative difference between the divine and the human. God says to Moses, 'you cannot see my face; for no one shall see me and live' (Exodus 33.20). And the author of John's Gospel, in his magisterial words on the incarnation, nevertheless records that 'No one has ever seen God' (John 1.18). In time, some came to believe that this was not just because of God's illimitable power but because of the consuming fire of his love.

Charles Wesley's genius is to locate himself and those who sing his hymn as Jacob, and God as Jesus. As we identify with Jacob, we confess to God that 'I need not tell thee who I am, my misery and sin declare'. Even so, 'thyself hast called me by my name'. The real question therefore is, 'who, I ask thee, who art thou? Tell me thy name and tell me now.' The biblical Jacob only eventually realized that he was struggling with God. We who sing this hymn know beforehand that our struggle is with God. The question for us is: what sort of God is God? Is he the God of Pat and Osama; or of Jeremiah and Hildegard and Mother Julian? Can he mend our broken lives and give us hope? As we wrestle with God, we demand:

> Yield to me now; for I am weak,
> but confident in self-despair;
> speak to my heart, in blessings speak,
> be conquered by my instant prayer;
> speak, or thou never hence shalt move,
> and tell me if thy name is Love.

Such a demand is impertinent, from the created to the creator; and foolish too, if one wishes to live. Unless, as both Wesley brothers experienced and believed, the answer to the question posed in this verse reveals the God whom Jesus taught and embodied, full of grace and truth. Indeed, the next verse declares passionately that we know with whom we wrestle:

> 'Tis Love! 'tis Love! Thou diedst for me!
> I hear thy whisper in my heart;

the morning breaks, the shadows flee,
pure, universal love thou art;
to me, to all, thy mercies move:
thy nature and thy name is Love.

No one sings this hymn nowadays. It is too long. It demands a measure of prayerful study that runs against our generation's desire for quick answers and instant gratification. Yet it demands to be read and prayed, as one of the glories of the evangelical revival.

'Wrestling Jacob' has much to teach us about God. We find God not on the surface but in the depths of life, in poetry more than in prose. If we are to prove his existence, it is not in the laboratory or in some other theoretical, abstract or speculative way, but in the depth of a relationship with him. God speaks to whom he will, to the shady and the tricksters, not just to the righteous; the self-righteous have a habit of mistaking their own congratulatory voice for his challenging and transforming summons, and so miss the mark. Since God is pure, universal love, we should be surprised by grace, not attempt to ration it in small amounts to those on our approved list. When and where Christians come across others who struggle with life's serious issues in faith, and hope, and love, then they should be able and willing, joyfully and not grudgingly willing, to relate that to Jesus and what he reveals of God's universal love.

We must explore the implications of these observations. We can begin by asking how we know that what 'Wrestling Jacob' points to is true.

When St Paul wrote of Jesus' resurrection to the Christian community in Corinth, he stated:

If Christ has not been raised, your faith is futile and you are still in your sins. Then those also who have died in Christ have perished. If for this life only we have hoped in Christ, we are of all people most to be pitied. (1 Corinthians 15.17–19)

Pope John XXIII, the holiest and greatest of twentieth-century Roman pontiffs, was once heard to say of Christian faith: 'Woe to us if all this is an illusion.' Even the saints know that faith is faith, and not factual knowledge. They could be wrong about life and death, faith and belief. But they are convinced that, if God is truly meaningful, the proof of it is in the dialogue of life. For Paul, life with God gives it meaning and holiness, overcoming our human tendency to selfishness and of missing the real point about things: in other words, it takes away our sins. God perfects us by his grace. In a relationship with God, we are bathed in and allured and challenged by love. The truth of that emerges in our daily relationship with him.

The wrong ideas of truth

Truth is a quest. One proviso, though: we should not confuse quest for process. A quest has a purpose. Some people wander in the desert of their inappropriate fantasies and behaviours with no intention of ever reaching the Promised Land, and a great number are in our churches and in the ordained ministry. Their commitment to process justifies them in sniffing about in the muck of their life without any real and honest desire for healing. Actually, if they found a therapist who could help them, or God's truth to guide and heal them, they would be resentful. They want to be admired or even pitied as victims, not forgiven and restored to life. They can usually fool enough people into paying attention to them, and so play the brave soldier struggling against great odds. They should be told to grow up, like the rest of us.

Truth is to be wrestled with, and found in the struggles of life. Our modern and modernist mistake, even as people of faith, is to interpret religion as valuable in so far as it conveys correct factual information about God which, as we believe it and live by it, puts us on the highway to heaven. Truth is not to be reduced to persuasive facts or correct information. Neither is it primarily about the existence or otherwise of a discrete visible or tangible thing: many of us have misguidedly bought into this notion that God is an object, to be proved or disproved.

The tendency of the modern world to interpret truth as factual accuracy may be all right as far as it goes, but it misses a range of meanings. In John's Gospel, Jesus talks of those who 'do what is true' (3.21), which resonates with a now old-fashioned understanding of truth as fidelity or faithfulness. We can hear echoes of that archaic interpretation in phrases like 'true to her convictions'. Truth has a rich significance that cannot be adequately conveyed by reducing it to factual accuracy.

So it is of little worth to interpret Jesus' approval of those who do what is true as a simple demand that people should get their ideas about God right.

Even intellectuals can tire of ideas, in the absence of contexts that give them meaning. One day in the summer of 1985, I flung the book I was reading the length of the courtyard where I was sitting under a tree, enjoying its shade during the middle of a hot Pakistani day. I was not, however, enjoying the book. My bad temper was not just due to heat and dust. As I described in chapter 3, in an attempt to improve my knowledge of Urdu, I had travelled to a small village in the Punjab where friends of friends lived. Few people there spoke English, and I have no Punjabi, so if I wanted to communicate verbally, in Urdu it had to be.

The book I was reading was by a distinguished Roman Catholic scholar and, in a broad sense, it was about religious truth. In other words, it ruminated on what is the case about this universe, especially given the context of many religions and ideologies that seem to give different answers to the fundamental questions of life, and sometimes even to pose dissimilar questions. I had taken it with me because I had to review it for an academic journal, but also because, as a Methodist minister, then responsible for two churches in the city of Leicester, I wanted to make sense of being in a village where everyone was a Muslim, far removed from my usual urban and religious setting. The book did not help me, at all.

In interpreting other faiths from a Christian perspective and in a positive light, the book declared that other religions produce saintly people. This is a useful point so far as it goes, but it does not go very far. It is tempting and trendy to suggest, implicitly or explicitly, that it does not matter very much what you believe or give your life to, so long as you are a good person. The book, to be fair, did not quite go that far, though, disoriented and deskilled as I was at the time, I was inclined to read it as doing so. I was irritated by the blithe assumption, not just of that writer but of many other authors of the time who wrote about religious pluralism, that the idea of the good is enough to make people good. For a few benign intellectuals, it may be. But goodness does not usually happen in a vacuum; nor does evil. Religious people have usually claimed that the stories and teachings of their faith mould the kind of people they become. To ignore them is to overlook the very things that empower people and enable goodness to flourish. Goodness is mostly rooted in strongly held convictions about who we are and what kind of universe we live in. If we seem embarrassed about these convictions, then it will seem to many others that our ethics are merely a form of amiability and spring from a desire to be agreeable, lacking any deep roots that will make them endure at all times and in all circumstances. Furthermore, such stories must be told, heard and acted upon in particular contexts that affect how we make them our own

Ideas, of course, can be presented as pure and unalloyed. We must, however, interpret stories. They can be wrenched out of their more obvious range of meanings to justify our own vision of the universe. The former British Prime Minister Margaret Thatcher's bizarre interpretation of the parable of the Good Samaritan to validate her monetary policy is an example of this: 'if opportunity and talent is unequally distributed, then allow-ing people to exercise that talent and opportunity means more inequality, but it means you drag up the poor people, because there are the resources to do so. No-one would remember the good Samaritan if he'd only had good intentions; he had money as well.'[1]

Claims to truth are indeed often disagreeably and exclusively framed, and spun in order to present specific points of view as the correct ones. Fundamentalists in all religions (and political parties) are often shrill in tone and unaware of or unconcerned about the immoral consequences of their judgements. They have not really understood truth at all, but have hammered out their assertions about God's nature and demands on the anvil of their own paranoia. Outsiders often fail to see that verbally or even physically violent fundamentalists often degrade, disenfranchise and sometimes even destroy their own co-religionists as a priority, before and more than they attack members of other faiths. The triumph of the Taliban in Afghanistan in the 1990s, and the sectarian violence against Shia Muslims urged by Sunni leaders of al-Qaida; the hate-filled statements of some North American Christian evangelists against those whose views are ironically more Christ-like than their own; and those supporters of the state of Israel who act as though any criticism of its policies, especially by other Jews, is an example of anti-Semitism: these provide examples of this troubling form of intra-faith, sectarian violence. It is encouraging (and often missed by the media and the current crop of neo-atheists who write against God and religion) that there are goodly and godly Jews, Christians and Muslims (and Hindus and others) who condemn their blinkered co-religionists who project their own violent and deranged ideas onto God and religion.

Clearly, it is not just a matter of how we present the truth we believe that is important, but the content we give to that truth. Narrow-minded and even wicked interpretations of reality remain narrow-minded and wicked, even if we dress them up in the garb of civility. They may be more decently expressed, but they are not thereby more decent. A local Baptist minister once told the Hindu owner of the corner shop near where I lived that he, the Hindu, would be going to hell for not believing in Jesus. Meanwhile he, the Baptist minister, was glad to know him and to buy produce from him. The fact that many religious people believe such exclusive and self-serving theologies does not make bad beliefs into good beliefs, or their words acceptable.

Moreover, even if we understand the context in which such stingy and niggardly views are expressed, that does not justify them. For example, the grinding poverty of many Muslim countries, and the political and economic dislocations that have resulted from western imperialism, may partially explain the attraction of Osama bin Laden's views to some Muslims, but they do not validate them. It may be that the influence of these views would wane if North American and European foreign policy sprang from a more authentically religious and moral vision than is the case, but that is only part of the solution. Indeed, many al-Qaida cells are made up of well-to-do Muslims, who may be angry on behalf of other Muslims but cannot claim themselves to be economically underprivileged. We need to confront and seek to change such contemptuous and contemptible views.

It is not just extremist views of truth that need to be challenged. Arguably, many respectable and longstanding views of truth are skewed to some extent. An interesting example of this can be found in recent official documents of the Roman Catholic Church about relations with other faiths, particularly with Jews. Since the reforms of the Second Vatican Council (1962–5), that church has been far more sympathetic to the claims of other faiths to have some knowledge of the truth. The harshness of its medieval claim that *extra ecclesiam, nulla salus* ('Outside the Church, there is no salvation') has been toned down, and different, more inclusive, voices from the past have been reclaimed and heard. Other Christian denominations have become 'separated brethren', and other faiths, particularly but not only Jews and Muslims, have been appreciated and cautiously affirmed. Nevertheless, the Roman Catholic Church remains convinced that it contains the fullness of salvation, and Pope Benedict XVI has made some recent, controversial and ill-managed attempts to fix this conviction in the minds of insiders and outsiders alike. In the minds of many members of the Roman Catholic Church it is, to put it rather crudely, the pick of the religious litter. Of course, it is not alone in regarding itself as such. For one of many examples, many Muslims regard other People of the Book (Jews, Christians, and sometimes members of other faiths) as having something of the truth, but not all of it. Should we live and let live, recognizing that it is a human trait to stand by what we believe as the best of things, or does this need challenging?

One argument for challenging it can be illustrated from church documents that struggle to make sense of conflicting claims to ultimate truth. The Roman Catholic documents *Dominus Iesus* (2000)[2] and *The Jewish People and Their Sacred Scriptures in the Christian Bible* (2001),[3] like virtually all committee publications, show signs of being the result of conflicting points of view. If those points of view settle around the issues of who is acceptable to God (which is what both Catholic and Protestant notions of salvation have obsessed about, to the exclusion of other interesting possibilities of its meanings), then what if an exclusive view were one day to win out and to insist on making its views plain to others, or even imposed on them? If that insistence were linked to political power and ambitions, then there could be the possibility of more wars justified by religion, of which there have surely been more than enough in human history. For this reason, among others, it may be wise to insist on looking at truth as something other than a matter of which human (or even divinely ordained) institution contains most or even all of it. There is also the point, already made in chapter 3, that religions are means of salvation and not ends in themselves, which many religious bureaucrats, who have invested greatly in the institution that supports them and gives them power and status, find it difficult and not in their temporal interest to admit.

This is where my hurling a book across a courtyard comes in. On the face of it, this was a curious thing to do, because it argued for rather a generous attitude towards truth. Although not written by the British philosopher John Hick, it represented the pluralist position that has become associated with his name.[4] That position maintains that all religions have a measure of access to the truth and should be regarded as equally valuable vehicles of salvation. Hick has described his Copernican shift from a theologically Ptolemaic view of reality. What he means by this metaphor is that, at first, he saw Christianity as the centre of the religious solar system, with other religions at varying distances of truthfulness from it. Then he replaced the Christian faith with Jesus. From there, he made the imaginative leap to put God at the centre. More recently, mindful of Buddhist and other faith-full objections to theistic language, he has written in Kantian terms of the really real as the heart of reality around which all things revolve.[5]

Hick and others have contrasted this positive and ideological interpretation of pluralism, which moves from recognizing the simple fact of religious diversity to embracing it is a veritable good, with exclusive and inclusive positions. Those who maintain exclusive ones claim that they are right (and saved) and others are wrong (and often damned). The inclusivist allows truth to others but only as the reflected glory of her own beliefs. So, for example, the Christian inclusivist will admit that members of other religions can be saved, because of the cosmic scope of Christ's work of salvation, not because non-Christians have access, through their own faith and beliefs, to something true and enduring. This division of views about the truths of other faiths into exclusive, inclusive and pluralist positions dominated the debate among religionists in the 1980s and 1990s, though it has recently seemed rather tired, overworked and running out of steam.[6]

The Power of the Truth

In 1985, a generous and pluralist interpretation of religious reality caused my fit of bad temper in a small village in the Punjab. Why on earth so? Surely I should have welcomed it as a distinct improvement upon the pious certainties of those who need to value the religious institution to which they belong by comparing others unfavourably with it. Actually, no. I applaud the sincerity and generosity of spirit of the author of the book I so abused, and of similar writers, but was and remain appalled by its excessively theoretical and abstract content. It was an excellent illustration of the wrongheaded notion that ideas are what really count, with an implicit assumption that they exist independently of any actual practitioners of them. I imagine the author would be appalled to have his work represented in this way, not least because he has made a great thing in later books about the importance of justice and peace, and the integrity of creation, and other good and worthy causes.

Still, look at it from my situation. There was I, a solitary, white Englishman in a far country, somewhat off base and insecure, talking basic Urdu with farmers and their families but reading this highfalutin theology and philosophy in English, and seeing nothing in it remotely connecting with the experiences I was having. I wished that the author could have been greeted, as I was, by the warm embrace of strangers. I would have liked him to have heard the rather scurrilous though light-hearted jokes made at the expense of the imam of the local mosque. It would have been good for the author to have talked with the young man who wanted to share his Muslim faith with me, because it had got him through the death of his beloved mother with a measure of hope and even joy. He might have been angered as I was by the instinctive and uninformed and widespread anti-Semitism in that village among people who had never met a Jew or been to Israel, and puzzled over where it came from, how to make sense of it, and how to defuse it of its venom. He would surely have noticed, as I did, how everyone took the importance of religion for granted yet were, shall we

151

say, very relaxed about performing many of the ritual require-
ments of their religion. As it was, the author of that book, for all
I could tell from reading it, would not have recognized a
Muslim, even if he fell over one.

So, if I were now to try to give some academic justification to
my book-destroying propensities of twenty years ago, it would
be something like this. The inclusive/exclusive/pluralist debate
championed by John Hick, and discussed in the flying book,
resolves the issue of religious truth by an ideological interpretation of pluralism, which looks more like an eccentric form of
western philosophical idealism than a distinctive characteristic
of the Semitic religious traditions from which many of its advocates spring. I wrote something in that vein for my review of it.

What I actually thought was rather more along the lines of:
'Get a life, man. Climb out of your head and look at the world
around you.'

In fact, since Christian (and Jewish and Islamic and many
other) thinkers have insisted that God is always greater than
humans can describe, one can and must attempt to get one's
ideas about God better than they could be, but it is a lost cause,
as well as an impertinence, to assume that one has them, and
therefore God, nailed down. Jesus told stories about God and
did deeds of power, which helped people to understand how
much more gracious God is than they have imagined or
deserved. This led people deeper into faith or fidelity. For Jesus,
truth was not primarily a thought or a belief or any kind of idea,
but a relationship with God and, through God, with others; and
its fruit is loyalty, commitment, and generosity of spirit.

The quest for truth

The wise in every generation and religion have believed that
truth is a relationship with God that reflects the divine qualities
that his grace bestows upon us. Fethullah Gülen, a contempo-

rary Turkish Muslim spiritual leader, has written: 'To be a truthful Muslim, one should avoid all kinds of hypocrisy and acts of blasphemy; one should surrender to God with utmost sincerity, and practice Islam with a consciousness of being in His presence and being watched by Him.'[7] Wilfred Cantwell Smith argued that God does not reveal himself as propositions, or as theologies, or as religions. He reveals himself as personal, to persons.[8] Surely Wilfred Cantwell Smith and Fethullah Gülen are at one here, encouraging us to be submitters to God, who we believe to have touched and transformed our lives. Yet too many Christian theologians think that God reveals theologies or Christianity; and too many Muslim scholars think that God reveals religious law or Islam. In truth, we have seen that these and all religions, and their component parts, are human constructions, human-made attempts to make sense of personal encounters with transcendent reality.

To be sure, these human constructions are responses to the divine initiative that seeks and saves the lost, and at their best they provide believers with homes for the human spirit. But they are not the truth; nor are their leaders uniquely qualified or divinely and exclusively authorized to interpret truth.

Truth is best seen as a quest. We grow into truth as we explore and develop our relationship with God. There are a number of indicators that the concept of truth as a journey is an instinctive human conviction. One is the remarkably widespread, almost universal, impetus of religious people to go on pilgrimage. Certain places are seen as particularly holy, including: Jerusalem for all three Abrahamic faiths, Rome for Christians, and Mecca and Medina for Muslims; and this list, which is far from exhaustive, could be extended to others of the world's faiths. People travel from far and wide, and at considerable financial and other personal cost, to visit such places. It is not just getting there that bestows merit, but often the sense of anticipation and preparation. There is also the remarkable sense of being part of an experience that transcends time and self. In 'Little Gidding', the last of his *Four Quartets*, T. S. Eliot wrote that 'you are here to kneel where prayer has been valid'. Little Gidding is a Huntingdonshire village visited by Eliot in 1936. A religious community had been founded there by Nicholas Ferrar in 1626, but it was broken up after King Charles I visited it in 1633, and again in 1646, fleeing Parliamentary troops at the end of the first Civil War. But, of course, the poem speaks to the universal impetus through the particular example. There are some places where many different sorts and conditions of people come to pray and, over the course of years, such spaces seem to become particularly sacred, suffused with holiness and a palpable sense of the presence of God.

Recently I took a group of university students to Turkey, and we saw many sites. Intriguingly, the place that touched many of us deeply was the house at Ephesus where the Virgin Mary is believed to have spent the last years of her life with the apostle John. When we arrived, there was a priest at prayer and also a Muslim woman (for Muslims, too, hold Mary in high regard). It did not seem to me that the aura of sanctity that the place conveys depended upon the factual accuracy of the reports of Mary's connection to the house. It was, rather, that here was a place where prayer has been valid for many years. It was truly a holy place.

A pilgrimage is a journey with religious meaning. The evangelist Luke conveys this point in his two-document contribution to the New Testament, his Gospel and the book of Acts. In Acts, Paul makes a number of journeys that gradually take the good news of Jesus from the Jewish capital of Jerusalem through the eastern Mediterranean region to Rome, the capital of the civilized world. Others too, like Philip and Peter, develop their understanding of God and the breadth of his love on the journeys they make. Luke clearly intends to convey a deeper meaning by his use of the motif of journeying than simply indicating the spread of the message of Jesus over a wide geographical area. Even his Gospel is full of journeys. After the visit of Gabriel telling her of the birth of Jesus, Mary visits Elizabeth. Jesus is born on a journey from Nazareth to Bethlehem, where his parents are forced to go to take part in a census. Two parables found only in Luke, the Good Samaritan and the Prodigal Son, arguably the two best-loved parables of all, are about journeys. In the first, a man is set upon by thieves on his way from Jerusalem to Jericho, ignored by two respectably religious passers-by and rescued by a third, dodgy, character. In the second, a man has two sons, the younger of whom wanders into a far land and back again to his father's love, whereas his brother stays at home but learns nothing important about generosity and kindness and need and hope. In Luke 9.51, Jesus 'set his face to go to Jerusalem', and took until the second half of chapter 19 to get there. After his death and resurrection, two disciples meet Jesus unawares on the road to Emmaus, and finally recognize him in the breaking of the bread.

Luke was profoundly aware that truth is a quest. You find God on a journey, deepening the insights of the relationship that you have with him. In the story of Emmaus (24.13–35), there is a poignant moment that points up the dashed expectations of the disciples. In telling the unrecognized Jesus about the crucifixion, they say to him, '. . . we had hoped . . .'. As they walk with him, Jesus restores their hope and helps them understand what has happened, and why, and what good can come from it. They finally recognize him in a characteristic action of hospitality, when he blesses and breaks bread with them; one that from earliest times became a part of the Church's liturgical life. Indeed, the story suggests that Jesus is most to be known in a life of worship: the study of the Hebrew Bible and participation in the Eucharist reveal God's grace and Jesus' own significant role in it. It is also a beguiling fact that only Cleopas is named of the two disciples. Is this Luke's way of writing the reader into the story? As we walk with Jesus, sometimes not recognizing or misunderstanding him, we can nevertheless catch a glimpse of his presence in the interpretation of Scripture and in the Lord's Supper, and find hope restored.

The parable of the Good Samaritan (Luke 10.25–37) is no more centred on the Samaritan than the Prodigal Son is mainly about that young rapscallion. The intriguing figure is the lawyer, the expert in religious procedure. It is characteristic of some people of faith to want things tied up and sorted. The concept of truth as quest does not appeal to them: they want things cut and dried. Luke tells us that the lawyer deliberately tested Jesus by asking him about how he can inherit eternal life. This lawyer was clear about the answer, but wanted to make sure Jesus had it right. (Yet the lawyer's views are of so little interest to Luke that he does not record them. Whatever they are, they are inappropriately fixed and final.) Jesus turned the question back to him. The lawyer mentioned love of God and others, quoting from the Bible to prove his point. Jesus congratulated him for giving 'the right answer'. The lawyer must have been discomfited. His question was supposed to make Jesus hop a bit, but the biter is bit, and it is he who is flustered and made to seem foolish. As a result, he overreaches, disastrously, by asking, 'And who is my neighbour?' Then Jesus tells the parable, and ends with a question of his own: 'Which of these three, do you think, was a neighbour to the man who fell into the hands of the robbers?'

The lawyer is in an impossible position. The way that the story is told makes it plain that the Samaritan was the neighbour. Yet Samaritans, who claimed descent from Jewish tribes, had eccentric religious views, with their own Temple on Mount Gerizim, and there was bad blood between them and Jews; they were not good neighbours. The priest and the Levite were more the lawyer's sort of person, for they had religious roles ascribed to them. Indeed, it may have been these roles that kept them from exercising pity, in case they became ritually impure. The Samaritan, who had no worries on that score since he was impure by dint of being himself, was moved with pity and acted on these instincts.

The lawyer could not bring himself to give a straightforward answer to Jesus' question. He did not say, 'The Samaritan.' Instead, presumably through clenched teeth, he responded, 'The one who showed him mercy.' Jesus no doubt took great pleasure in having the last word: 'Go and do likewise.' In other words: 'Go and be like a Samaritan; at least, like the Samaritan of this story.'

The story characteristically has a sting in its tale. Jesus was full of surprises. Those who think they have a handle on truth find that they do not. According to Matthew, Jesus said to the chief priests and elders of the people that 'the tax-collectors and the prostitutes are going into the kingdom of God ahead of you' (21.31). This is because they did not believe 'the way of right-eousness' taught by John the Baptist: it did not come to them in a guise they were able to recognize, any more than they could believe it when taught by Jesus. They were not seekers after truth, because they thought it was already their possession.

There are occasional and rather touching indications that Jesus himself, though he knew his Father in heaven to be the God of surprises, was surprised into truth. For example, when a Roman centurion sent friends to Jesus to ask him to heal his slave, this Gentile soldier showed faith in and recognition of his authority that the chief priests and elders did not. Luke tells us:

> When Jesus heard this he was amazed at him, and turning to the crowd that followed him, he said, 'I tell you, not even in Israel have I found such faith.' When those who had been sent returned to the house, they found the slave in good health. (Luke 7.9–10)

It was not that Jesus did not expect to find faith in Israel. He did, just as we expect to find faith among Christians but might sometimes wish that it were more generously and joyfully and lovingly and hopefully expressed. It has proven easy for Christians throughout the centuries to point a finger at the Jews, or their leaders, as the object of Jesus' anger and judgement. In this way, they have managed to avoid seeing the finger point at them. Yet Jesus lived and died a Jew; he was steeped in the religious stories and customs of his people, and spoke out of that context. If, occasionally, one has the impression that the evangelists (who wrote within and for people who lived in other geographical contexts) are scoring points against Jews, it is foolish to think of Jesus in that way. Rather, the things he saw and condemned in his own tradition of faith are universals: self-righteousness; spiritual one-upmanship; narrowing the mercies of God to self and the like-minded; pompous and overconfident religious leaders; mistaking means for ends; a lack of humour; and so on. Behind all these indications of bad faith lies a common problem: the smug satisfaction of those who think they have got the point but who have not.

How God deals with the capacity of his human children to tame and domesticate or else to ignore and deny him is the subject of the parable of the Prodigal Son; for it is the (in some ways) God-like father who is the interesting figure in this story. The emphasis in this and the previous two parables, all recorded in Luke 15, is upon the lost sheep, the lost coin and the lost sons being found, though there is some question as to whether the conventional elder son has realized just how lost he is.

The younger son asks for his share of the property, then leaves home and squanders it. Eventually he returns, not because he is sincerely repentant, but because he has nowhere else to go. When he, a Jewish lad, reaches rock-bottom and finds himself working with pigs, he comes to himself: he realizes how well-fed his father's servants are, so he makes up a tear-jerking speech about being willing to be a servant, and goes home. He cannot get all of his sob-story out before his father has embraced and kissed him, and welcomed him back.

Those who feel sorry for the elder son should not waste their pity. When his younger brother took his share of the inheritance, he also took his. Accepting it before the father died was scandalous according to the social conventions of the day: it was equivalent to wishing the old man were dead. So here we have a man who took his father's money, stayed at home and, when his brother came home, ignored his own wrongdoing, concentrating only on the alleged sins of his sibling, and sulked. He accused his brother of squandering money on prostitutes: how would he have known this, since he did not have the courage to flaunt his own failings, but kept up the appearance of a dutiful son by staying at home and working the family business? (Moreover the NRSV's translation of 'dissolute living' in verse 13 is wrong. The Greek means 'living wastefully', so the precise way in which the younger boy frittered away his money is not known to us, any more than it was to his brother.) The elder son slanders his brother. His scornful reference to 'this son of yours' reminds the reader of the lawyer's unwillingness to directly name the Samaritan, as though he were superior to him. He then humiliates and insults his father by refusing to attend the party, at which, as the elder son, he should have been present with his father to greet the guests. If the younger brother is a sort of teenage bubblehead, there is a chilling air of cold calculation about the older lad.

The father is the most scandalous figure of all: he is old enough to know better than to indulge his two feckless sons; he should, presumably, have beaten and maybe disinherited them instead. Where, one wonders, are the mother and sisters to add some sense and sensibility to this dysfunctional family?

It is not because of what the son has done that he is welcomed back, but because of who the father is: a man of illimitable love, who cares nothing about what the neighbours might say or any other social nicety, if it stands in the way of his love for his boys. Because of this there is hope for the older lad, too, that there is grace to cover all his sins, even though he is reluctant to admit, possibly even to recognize, that he has any to confess.

We can take it that the father's guests would have been amused at but also shocked by their neighbours' public washing of dirty laundry. Presumably, Jesus' original hearers would also have enjoyed and laughed at this story. They would have been titillated by the problems of this well-off family, with money to spend on fine clothes and food. They would no doubt have tut-tutted over the problems that beset many people in close family relations, and which some of them may have thought were made even worse if you were among the idle rich and had the hope of money to spend – but, usually, only after a father died and the will was read.

Humour, of course, is part of the attraction of Jesus' teachings, though some religious people do not or cannot appreciate or even see it, having literal minds and loveless hearts. Indeed, to tell the truths of the universe in the form of stories is a dangerous enterprise. You have to hope that people will not be diverted from their substance to concentrate on the peripheral and unimportant. You have to trust that, for at least some people who hear, the penny will drop. You have to allure, not coerce. You have to give space and hope that things will work out, as the father did to his two sons. If you have a Pat or an Osama on your hands, it may be that they can never get it, even with all the space and time in the world and beyond. Yet, if the father's love for his wayward sons is at all like God's for his human children, there is always hope if never certainty.

At any rate, we write the truths we hold about the universe in our own lives. Since God is a player in them, captivating, loving, forgiving and renewing us, there is always the hope that we will come to our senses, and respond in love to his love.

The journey towards truth – beginnings

Journeys start from somewhere. Beginnings matter, because they shape who we become, for good or ill. Had the waiting father's sons been born into poverty, the forms of their rebellion would have taken different shapes, as would their opportunities to respond to grace.

The Power of the Truth

Many Christians can locate three important beginnings to their faith. One is the occasion or occasions when habitual or received faith became their own in meaningful ways. Another is Christianity's historical beginning in the life of Jesus and the stories of the earliest days of the faith, recorded in the New Testament. A final starting point is the church in which their faith is rooted.

I read Enid Blyton's *The Children's Life of Christ* when I was five years old. I was hooked: not so much on the other works of Miss Blyton, though I read tales about the Famous Five and the Secret Seven voraciously for a time. Rather, the stories in that particular book about the teaching of Jesus captivated me. They still do, though the stiff upper-lip, 'Are you sitting comfortably?' style of that author no longer holds my attention in the way that once it did. Still, I am eternally grateful to her, to use that overworked adverb in a meaningful sense. Of course, we all have different beginnings for the kindling of our faith. For some people there are incidents, trivial or spectacular, that can be recalled and recounted. Some self-publicists fall into the temptation of assuming that something extravagant has to happen to everyone for their faith to be authentic, as if God does not speak in the still, small voice but only through the spiritual equivalent of a tsunami. Thus, and ironically, they make a good work out of their faith, in ways that would not have been approved by St Paul, among others. For many people, the beginning of their faith is more like the moment they began to talk: long-forgotten in the mists of time, but remembered in the overwhelmingly important consequences for who they have become and are becoming.

Another beginning for Christians is the life of Jesus and its consequences. There have been a number of quests for the historical Jesus in the Enlightenment period. Nineteenth- and early twentieth-century writers about his life often found a Jesus who appealed to their temperament and character. In Renan's book (see page 51 above), Jesus looks suspiciously like Renan himself: rather self-consciously romantic, sentimental and manipulative. In his famous work *The Quest of the Historical Jesus* (first published in German in 1906), Albert Schweitzer pointed out that very many of Jesus' 'biographers' had looked down a well and seen their own face stare back at them. He also managed, with a remarkable absence of irony, to describe a Jesus of his own imagination. Truth to tell, that has, to some extent, always been the case when people write about Jesus. Each of the evangelists has his own spin on the story of Jesus, and it is tempting and probably accurate to infer things about each of the evangelists from what they wrote about him. For example, it would not be surprising to find that Luke was suspicious of wealth, remarkably free and easy in the presence of women, and a great raconteur: just like his portrait of Jesus.

Even so, we have already seen that one of Jesus' extraordinary knacks is the capacity not to conform to and justify our glib certainties. Instead, he shocks and surprises us, not least in the stories that he tells, which subvert many of our received opinions and are intended to jolt us into more inclusive and generous and open-ended responses than we have hitherto learned and lived by.

If Schweitzer sounded the death-knell of this first stage of the quest for the historical Jesus, Rudolph Bultmann and other German theologians of the twentieth century buried it in a deep grave. They cast serious doubts on how much we can know about the historical Jesus. Bultmann assured us that we deal with the Christ of faith. He had a good point in emphasizing this, even though his scepticism (and even that of his disciples who initiated a new quest that was very slightly more open to a positive assessment of the evidence of what Jesus said and did) now looks needlessly overdone. We know a great deal more about Jesus and Paul than we do about most other figures of the ancient world, and the criticism made by many New Testament scholars that the accounts are not value-free but laden with interpretative freight only shows just how many of them are philosophers or textual scholars; or at any rate are not historians who know that this is true of every (well, of very, very many) assessment of figures of the past.

Still, Bultmann's point is good because it makes us ask what the purpose of accessing the historical Jesus is. Many Christians make the false assumption that it is easy to know what Jesus said, did and thought, and that these can be applied directly to their own situations. This can be illustrated from the views of many people who wear WWJD (What Would Jesus Do?) bracelets and articles of clothing. No doubt I have been unlucky, but my few encounters with people who so adorn themselves lead me to believe that nothing Jesus could say would surprise them, and (to fall for a moment into the trap they habitually do) that he would have been more than surprised, but also gob-smacked and indignant, at what they foist on him. They have his views all sorted, whether on abortion, sex before marriage, homosexuality, which political party to vote for, or some other thing about which, the Gospels indicate, he said little or nothing.

In reality, even if we were able to know the timetable of Jesus' life in detail: so what? The past is a foreign country and needs interpreting. We are not first-century Jews, and, if some time-machine landed us there, we would be bewildered, not just by a different language, but by many cultural assumptions that divide us one from the other. Our vocation is obedience in our own time and setting. We have to work hard at understanding what we can usefully learn from the past, and must rely upon scholars, preachers and others to help us. For example, what we know of fathers from Jesus' day and culture is that, loving and caring though they were, they were more authoritative and authoritarian than we typically experience. This points up how surprising the story of the waiting father is, who had power that custom would have allowed and expected him to use to punish recalcitrant children, but did not use it.

Christianity is not to be absolutely identified with the teachings of Jesus. Faith is about how individuals and communities relate to them, and to him, and to God, in the contexts in which they find themselves. To be sure, the life and teachings of Jesus provide the major resource by which Christians can measure the truth of our own faithful responses. But our journey makes us deal with different issues than the four evangelists, Peter, Paul and others. We are not antiquarians, reviving a sacred past as though it were a golden age that can and should be replicated in all times and places. This pining after a past ideal society or historical moment is a characteristic and, to be frank, a fault of people in many religions, not just of some Christians. For example, it is curious and unconvincing to hear Muslims talk nostalgically of the golden age of the first four caliphs (who were successors to the Prophet Muhammad as political leaders of the Islamic community from 632 to 661) when, in reality, it was a period of intermittent civil war, when three of those caliphs were murdered. We value our heritage when we speak the truth about it, warts and all, not when we create a fictitious ideal that is unconvincing to any who give it a moment's thought.

Because religions are lived by human beings, who are not only sinful but limited by particular contexts of time and space, it is obvious that the ideals of religious communities are compromised by actual practices. We need to be aware of this when we look at the Christian community that we call home, because the third beginning for the faith of many Christians is the church to which they belong. This is so for many of those attracted to Christ; but not for all. A few individuals like Simone Weil, though entranced by a particular denomination, keep at a deliberate distance from it. Some people, hurt or unpersuaded by the teachings of their denomination of birth, move to another. As it happens, the church in which I presently worship is full of people who describe themselves, semi-humorously, as 'recovering' Catholics, or Methodists, or some other denomination. Speaking, as one who has made this transfer, to other such refugees, it is telling how many of them still feel some kind of bond with their original denomination, even if it seems like dealing with an abusive parent. There are also individuals who move out of one religion to an entirely different one, though even some of these are more influenced by their past than they care to admit. I remember one conversation with a Muslim convert whose views about God seemed little altered from those of the Scottish Calvinism of his birth: he had, as it were, changed his religion but not his faith. And some people come late, out of no clear religious background, to embrace a church as their own.

For most of us who have pledged our troth to a religious institution, we owe it our loyalty, though not in any mindlessly accepting way. It is not perfect, but it is ours.

Take Methodism as an example, which is the denomination that has formed me. Although I now attend a United Churches of Christ congregation, its convictions do not speak to me, or irritate me, or stir my heart, as much as Methodism's do. This is not because Methodism is objectively superior to other Christian denominations, but because it is ineradicably part of who I am. Many English people who appreciate classical music love Elgar because his music, while owing much to German influences, speaks powerfully of England. His near contemporary, Richard Strauss, may be the greater composer (he certainly had the greater range) but his music does not move me as does Elgar's. As another great English composer, Ralph Vaughan Williams, said: 'I believe that one's own community, one's own language, customs and religion, are essential to our spiritual health. Without local loyalty, there can be nothing for the wider issues to build on.' Just so: for people of a particular faith, as well of a specific nationality.

It is obvious that British Methodism is in a parlous state, as we have already seen. Whenever I used to hear or read the addresses of Presidents of Conference given at the end of their year of office, I was always intrigued to discover all the signs of hope that abound in Methodist churches throughout the land. I was never sure if this was a case of the general whistling in the dark to keep up the spirits of his troops, or if church leaders and I inhabited parallel universes where decline in one must be interpreted as success in the other. There is no truthfulness in living within an institution and being dishonest about it.

Nor is there any value or honour in not knowing or ignoring or subverting what it stands for. 'Wrestling Jacob' is an example of the theology of Methodism, which, for the most part, and guided by John Wesley and the hymns of Charles, rejected the widespread Calvinism[9] of the day in favour of Arminianism. In other words, it placed no limits on the range of God's love, and rejected readings of Scripture and of tradition that identified a particular and small group of saved over against the much larger association of the damned. Many churchgoers today shop around for a spiritual home, far more than used to be the case. This means that many churches contain people with very different understandings of God, and such diversity can often be fruitful and enriching. But that is no reason to play down what the denomination stands for. Indeed, it is urgently important to spell out its core ideals, and make sure that its local preachers, deacons and presbyters identify with them. For example, Methodists baptize infants because they believe that God's love precedes, and is more significant than, our human response to it. They sing of that love. I found it odd, when I taught in a theological college, that a number of ordinands expressed their refusal to follow Methodist practice, and would only baptize those who were eager or willing to make a statement of faith. I would sometimes suggest that they should join the Baptists, who stand for different views than our own, some of which we must disagree with in friendly fashion. Understandably, some students were hurt and upset by my suggestion. Still, if you stand as guardian at the gate of the institution, your job is not to be a bouncer keeping out the riff-raff, but to ensure that those who are set in authority within it should know and identify with what it stands for. Although there are some logical tensions in his views about infant baptism, Mr Wesley accepted it as the practice of Scripture: the New Testament equivalent of circumcision, a sign of entry into the covenant promises of God. He would not have approved of the views of my students, for whom God's free gift was less important than publicizing human responses to it.

Local loyalty, to use Vaughan Williams' words, does not mean that we identify our institution with the truth, to the exclusion of the views of all other ways of faith. But it does recognize that we start from somewhere to grow into the people we must become. Roots matter.

The journey towards truth – alternative visions of truth

It is plain that John Wesley's strongly Arminian views were quite different from George Whitfield's Calvinist convictions. The modern ecumenical movement has, of course, meant that Christian leaders and others now have an opportunity of airing and sharing their differences and their points of agreement. There are still considerable divergences between and within the mainstream denominations and other Christian communities, but there has been a great deal of progress in the last century or so, with the founding of the World Council of Churches in 1948, and of national Councils of Churches. The Roman Catholic reforms of the Second Vatican Council from 1962 to 1965 also forwarded this spirit of co-operation and openness. Much of the progress has been in cordiality and courtesy (though Wesley could sometimes express profound differences with surprising sensitivity), but there have also been (often cautious) attempts to overcome theological and ecclesiological differences, often stemming from the Reformation period.

Intra-Christian conviviality is one thing. But our contemporary world is mapped on a wider canvas, and there is also the question of other religions and their competing claims to truth and to the loyalty of humankind.

Recent attempts at inter-religious dialogue go back further than many people know, at least to the World's Parliament of Religions in 1893, held that September as part of the World Columbian Exposition in Chicago. The Second Vatican Council began a process that has vastly improved Roman Catholic relations with Jews, while Protestants (and not so much, but to some extent, the Orthodox Churches) have also set about mending fences with other religions in our post-colonial and post-modern age.

It is unwise to play down differences between religions about how we define and relate to the transcendent dimension to life. For all the connections between the Abrahamic faiths, Jews, Christians and Muslims are still divided over crucial issues, such as the meaning of Jesus. Broadly put: he is unimportant to and mostly ignored by Jews; crucially important to Christians; and relatively important to Muslims, who describe him in ways that seem only vaguely familiar and agreeable to Christians. It is possible to overlook such problems and to concentrate on areas of agreement, such as the need for us all to live decent and peaceable lives. Hence the present focus of many interfaith practitioners upon the 'dialogue of life' which, though a worthy aspiration, can sometimes make us seem as though we do not stand for anything very much. It can also pay no attention to crucial questions about how we are empowered to live such exemplary lives.

In interfaith circles it is often a matter of much bewilderment and amusement to others that there are so many Methodist participants. One reason for this is the Methodist commitment to Mr Wesley's vision of social holiness. In his Sermon 110 on 'Free Grace', he interpreted the doctrine of predestination to mean that God's grace was only for the few and that the great majority of humankind is condemned to death. He came down hard on the doctrine of predestination, not because he was of a sentimental disposition and inclined to see good in all people (except stern Calvinists). Rather, he wrote: 'It overturns both his [God's] justice, mercy, and truth. Yea, it represents the most Holy God as worse than the devil; as both more false, more cruel, and more unjust.' He observed that 'this uncomfortable doctrine directly tends to destroy our zeal for good works'. In other words, it militated against holiness for, as Wesley put it:

> if a sick man knows that he must unavoidably die or un-avoidably recover, though he knows not which, it is not reasonable for him to take any physic at all. He might justly say (and so I have heard some speak, both in bodily sickness and in spiritual) 'If I am ordained to life, I shall live; if to death, I shall die. So I need not trouble myself about it.' So directly does this doctrine tend to shut the very gate of holiness in general, to hinder unholy men from ever approaching thereto, or striving to enter in thereat.[10]

What if one were to see such holiness elsewhere than in Christians? It is because Methodists can see it working through Jews, Muslims, Hindus and others that many are involved, hopefully and joyfully, in interfaith dialogue.

They would have Mr Wesley's approval. He did not have much to do with people of other faith, and could occasionally give vent to the conventional and dismissive judgements of his day. But not always, as his sermon number 106 'On Faith' reveals.[11] His text was from Hebrews 11.6: 'Without faith it is impossible to please him [God]'. Talking of some people of other faith, he observed that:

> many of them, especially in the civilized nations, we have great reason to hope, although they lived among heathens, yet were quite of another spirit; being taught of God, by his inward voice, all the essentials of true religion. Yea, and so was that Mahometan, an Arabian, who, a century or two ago, wrote the Life of Hai Ebn Yokton. The story seems to be feigned; but it contains all the principles of pure religion and undefiled.

Wesley was correct in believing that Hayy Ibn Yaqzan, the hero of a story, was not a historical figure. His story, as elaborated by the twelfth-century Iberian Muslim philosopher Ibn Tufayl, contributed to the debate among medieval Muslim philosophers and theologians about the nature of the lonely soul, including whether some people could acquire by dint of intellectual thought and analysis and intuition what others learned from God's direct revelation in the Qur'an and the Hadith (authoritative sayings of Muhammad). The hero grows up alone on an equatorial island, and displays faith in that context.[12]

According to Wesley, Hayy Ibn Yaqzan learned 'all the principles of true religion'. Characteristically, Wesley ascribed that to the 'inward voice': the mystical vision that he himself had experienced, and its transforming consequences. Wesley did not feel the need to be defensive about Christianity, and was prepared to recognize 'pure religion and undefiled' wherever he found it. Quite so. If we see holiness and call it diabolical, we have presumably committed the unforgivable sin (Mark 3.20–30); unforgivable, not because of the hardness of God's heart, but because the hardness of our own has made us unaware of our unnecessarily and inappropriately harsh judgements and the need to repent of them.

We noted earlier in this chapter that recent theological and philosophical attempts to place other religions and their adherents within or outside the scope of God's saving love have become tired and stale. While we wait for more fruitful ones to emerge we could do much worse than hold fast to what we have learned from John Wesley. We can recognize the authenticity of the quest for holiness wherever we find it and, unlike him (for we live alongside significant numbers of Jews, Muslims, Hindus and others), we can work with such adventurous spirits to mend the world. If our new theologies of religion were to arise from this common action and interaction, from a 'dialogue of life' that does not shirk difficult questions, they might prove rich and productive indeed.

The end of truth

The American philosopher Richard Rorty, who died in 2007, an atheist and sceptic about absolute truth, once observed that truth is 'what my friends let me get away with saying'. But he also said: 'My sense of the holy is bound up with the hope that some day my remote descendants will live in a global civilization in which love is pretty much the only law.'

His scepticism about any objective content to truth is found within some contemporary strands of religion, though mostly only those that have had a strong contact with Enlightenment values.[13] One of its most recent Christian expressions is non-realism, associated with the British Cambridge philosopher Don Cupitt, who has himself been influenced by Rorty's 'anti-representationalism'. For Rorty, things we believe are not copies of any divine eternal world 'up there', but tools. Non-realists hold that knowledge is not objectively true, but shaped by the human mind. We have useful ideas about our world, not a divinely given truth about the world. If we are to use the language of God, it is to know that God is a poetic way of talking about beauty and our other highest values.

There is nothing new under the sun: non-realism is the by-blow of European philosophical scepticism, indebted to Feuerbach's conviction that 'the concept of God is nothing more than the projection into the heavens of the idealized human essence'. In Great Britain, non-realism is promoted by the Sea of Faith network. Its 'mission is to explore and promote religious faith as a human creation. The Network has no creed. It welcomes people from all faith and non-faith traditions.'[14]

Just as Arnold's poem refers to the 'melancholy, long, withdrawing roar' of faith, so there is a sense of depressed and depressing retreat about non-realism. It is a gentle and genteel way for those who have lost their faith to find the way out of their denominational back door. Nobody should underestimate the power of art and aesthetics in religion, nor the sense of regret and loss for those for whom meaningful words and other artefacts have lost their power. Still, non-realists should not be as surprised as many of them are when mainstream Christians and other religious people think of them as the Trojan Horse within the city of faith. Moreover, theirs is a very highbrow, middle-class enterprise, offering to poor and destitute people only a smidgeon of the benefits of faith: poetry without justice is a poor choice. Again, as is often the case with even very intelligent people who have been influenced by the values of modernity and postmodernity, one is left wondering why crucial issues are reduced to either/or instead of both/and. Why is religion either a human or a divine creation? Surely it can be credibly presented as a human creation in response to the divine self-revelation that empowers us to love goodness as well as beauty, and to work with God to become like God.

According to John's Gospel, Jesus said that 'you will know the truth, and the truth will make you free' (8.32). People are often scared of the truth, because it shows them in a poor light. So, to use John's language, we prefer darkness to light. Our assumption is that God, if God exists, is out to get us for all our faults and frailties. We certainly do well to ponder Jesus' words that 'those who do what is true come to the light, so that it may be clearly seen that their deeds have been done in God' (John 3.21). Occasionally, John's somewhat dualistic preference for light and darkness, good and evil, truth and falsehood, is depressing to those of us who inhabit the grey areas of life more often than we should and would. The teaching of Jesus, and the experience of many Christians since, is that, if we risk exposing ourselves to the light, we shall be drawn into its healing power: 'that sight of the Most Fair / Will gladden thee, but it will pierce thee too'.[15] T. S. Eliot wrote that 'human kind cannot bear very much reality'.[16] If so, it is not because God does not touch our lives with hope. But hope is not knowledge, and so truth is a quest. Truth is a relationship with God, begun now but fulfilled as we deepen our relationship with him. The Church's job is not to fill us with the notion that truth is our assent to a number of propositional statements, or a narrow and bigoted sense of moral outrage. Nor is it to give way to any passing fancy that would remove from religion its sense that God is, loves, and relates to us, for, as Dean Inge wryly observed, 'whoever marries the spirit of this age will find himself a widower in the next'.

The Church's major task is to resource people for that journey towards the fullness of truth, where 'Death will be no more; mourning and crying and pain will be no more, for the first things have passed away' (Revelation 21.4). Truth turns out to be not only what is learned on the religious quest, but God, who is its end.

6

Journeys End in Lovers' Meeting

Religion is humankind's most long-established and well-tested quest. It offers people an understanding of life's meaning and insights into life's last great adventure of death. Yet we have seen that mainstream religions have come under sharp criticism in the contemporary world, particularly in Western Europe. This criticism has been made easier by modernity's transformation of religion into a choice, rather than a given layer of society. Modernity also harshly objectified transcendent reality: in other words, God also became more of a 'thing' to be either accepted or rejected and less of a dimension of daily life to be taken for granted.

Still, in many other parts of the world, religion still flourishes, for good or ill; and even in Europe it survives, though sometimes under threat and, in some places, with a whiff of the second-rate about it. It is a human invention, at its best manufactured by humans in response to divine grace, and its capacity for great good or great evil or stupendous banality is dependent upon the creative imagination of people who interpret it in their daily living. Religion can be used to empower or oppress, to heal or to destroy, to advantage certain people or for the common good, to build society up or to tear it apart. The social sciences provide helpful ways of understanding the contexts within which religion operates. However, some of their earliest significant intellectuals were too sceptical and went too far in assuming that their academic discipline located religion's origins in the human mind, or in theories of social order, or in some other entirely secular explanation.

Ironically, some fervently religious people have facilely bought into modernist assumptions. For example, Christians who deny evolution because of the accounts of creation in Genesis or Muslims who claim that the Qur'an predicts modern scientific advances are wasting their time and misunderstand the point of what they believe in. The Bible and the Qur'an were revealed in a premodern world: they are works of religious genius, not scientific tracts.

The truth of religion lies in its conviction that there is a transcendent dimension to life, beyond the usual senses. That dimension, which Christians call God or some other equivalent word in their language (as do other, but not all, people of faith), speaks to us, and draws us into a relationship that gives our lives hope and meaning. The mystics are particularly good witnesses to this relationship, but their experience of God is different only in degree and not in kind from that of the rest of us. God loves all whom God has made.

If it is true, to refer once again to Charles Wesley's hymn 'Wrestling Jacob', that we have 'all eternity to prove thy nature and thy name is Love', what does this mean in a world of religious conflict, economic disparities, and bitter divisions over such issues as abortion and human sexuality? How, if at all, does the context of eternity give meaning to our religious obligations here and now? To such issues we must turn in this last chapter.

The beauty of holiness

We begin in worship. Where else can we, as a response to divine grace and goodness?

A story is told in the *Russian Primary Chronicle* of how, towards the end of the tenth century, Prince Vladimir of Kiev sent his followers to various places in order to find true religion. They tried Islam and also western Christian worship. Then they came to Constantinople and attended the Divine Liturgy in the Church of the Holy Wisdom. Finally, they had found what they wanted:

> We knew not whether we were in heaven or on earth, for surely there is no such splendour or beauty anywhere upon earth. We cannot describe it to you: only this we know, that God dwells there among humans, and that their service surpasses the worship of all other places. For we cannot forget that beauty.[1]

Of course there is an apologetic and even confrontational tone to this account, understandable in the context of its day. Yet it is a poignant illustration of the power and the purpose of worship. Worship inspires believers to live with God in God's world, providing resources not just for the mind and the heart but also for our aesthetic sensibilities.

In a world of religious differences, Vladimir's emissaries found truth in worship. There, they felt the presence of God. The tendency of all religions to split and splinter means that we should not exaggerate any uniformity of religion; or of worship, which has sometimes provided the source of religious divisions. Even so, religions provide acts of communal worship that are traditionally considered at least as important as private worship. Our modern capacity for choice – for we have more choices even than Vladimir's emissaries – and our emphasis upon an individualism that would have been meaningless to them, can undermine the purpose of worship when it becomes not about beauty but about us.

God speaks to individuals in worship and in mystical experiences, but draws them out of themselves into something splendid and beautiful. The many kinds of Christian worship that have developed through time can be something beautiful for God, or else cheapened by human selfishness or triviality. Orthodox worship, such as the story of the prince's ambassadors recounts, can be majestic and awe-inspiring, or tired and done in a way that removes the laity from any participation worth mentioning. Roman and Anglo-Catholic worship can be colourful and dramatic, or distractingly dependent upon tat pretending to be art. The blessedness of Quaker silence can be filled with the trivial effusions of the self-indulgent. And so on.

Worship is not best or adequately thought of as a way of affirming its 'co-ordinators'. I am surely not alone in wanting to throw a hymnbook at preachers and officiants who tinker gracelessly with components of worship, saying something along the lines of 'Now may the grace of our sweet Lord Jesus, and the love of the great and wise God, and fellowship in the uniting Holy Spirit, be with you, those whom you love, and the whole world, this day, tomorrow and for evermore.' At such moments, among the many things I mutter under my breath are 'Just say it. It's not about you and your piety.' Nor is worship intended to be an opportunity for other individuals to parade their faith or godliness in public, or for ministers to demonstrate their democratic credentials by letting anyone or chosen ones read Scripture or a favourite poem or play the piano or guitar or banjo. Sometimes, there is a thin boundary between this kind of inappropriate privatization of religion, which encourages us to do self-affirming things in public space, and the desire to involve all of us, and our gifts, as an offering to God. If we cannot tell when we have crossed that divide, we are in trouble.

Worship is about God, and about developing the relationship that we have with him. Worship offers us the comfort of resting in well-known words, and the challenge of responding to them when they strike us afresh with new insights. It is about seeing through the preacher to God: ministers should be windows not mirrors; they should not get in the way. If we are to hear of the preacher's life, it should be because it usefully and relevantly illustrates faith and hope and love, not because it is of absorbing interest to her and therefore, she foolishly assumes, must also be to us.

Worship is not primarily a teaching tool, for it is meant to be more inspiring than didactic. Nevertheless, from the beginnings of Methodism, hymn-singing has both stirred Methodist hearts and fed Methodist minds. There is not much sustenance in many modern choruses, which are flavoured with an excess of saccharine substituting for love. Many of them are also full of bad theology, so that we are diminished by what we settle for instead of built up by embracing the riches we could have. To be sure, much traditional, old-fashioned worship is dated and often performed so that it is needlessly boring, but mindless and inferior entertainment is not a respectable or responsible alternative to it.

We have already noted that there is a tendency for some scholars of liturgy and, especially, spirituality, to tinker with old and, for some, much-loved hymns. To a point, this is a reasonable enterprise. In 'Wrestling Jacob', Charles Wesley originally wrote that 'to all, thy bowels move', reflecting the eighteenth-century conviction that the bowels were the seat of pity and of the gentler emotions. To sing or read that now might stir other emotions in the congregation asked to do so, and 'mercies' seems a tolerable substitute. Some well-intentioned adjustments effect more changes than they intend or should. 'Hark! The herald angels sing' has a better chance of capturing our attention than 'Hark how all the welkin rings, Glory to the King of Kings' – 'welkin' meaning 'heaven'. Yet William Cummings, who changed Wesley's words towards the end of the nineteenth century to fit them to Mendelssohn's music, has contributed to the now widespread notion that the angels sang to mark the birth of the redeemer, which Scripture does not say and which Charles Wesley did not mean to convey.[2]

The current cottage industry of changing hymns is usually to void them of their patriarchal and other unworthy content. Enthusiasts for this enterprise should bear two things in mind. First, all of our hymns were written by fallible humans, some no doubt more at fault than others, so none of them is perfect. If we are to make the judgement that some imperfections are so outstanding that they need to be removed, we should bear in mind that we have made a choice that enables others to see our own prejudices and fallibility. These can be gleaned not just from what we have removed but from what we have allowed to remain. It is a brave thing to be a tinkering liturgist – or fool-hardy. A second point is that, while we can applaud the aims and intent of such practices, we can also mourn the way in which they are sometimes done. The soul needs good theology to flourish, but it also needs poetry. Modern hymn writers and editors may have a more up-to-date understanding of God than, say, Wesley and Watts, but they do not always display their brilliance in choosing words and how to put them together in ways that make the heart sing, even when the mind occasionally has reservations.

Some denominations, congregations and individuals also extend their corrections to prayers and other parts of the liturgy. Here again, the intentions can be good yet the finished product can be unfitting. The grumbles in some quarters about 'political correctness' are sometimes from people who need to widen their understanding of God's love. But occasionally they are a clumsy way of expressing a sense of real loss when the cadences and rhythms of life's complexities are translated into worship with an exaggerated and prosaic certainty about right and wrong. Occasionally, worshippers feel that they are reading something less like a psalm or a hymn and more like a supermarket shopping or a to-do list.

Some congregations are encouraged to substitute 'Mother' or 'Creator' for 'Father' in prayers, very occasionally even in the Lord's Prayer. Many people feel uneasy at tinkering about with Scripture. Nevertheless, some New Testament writers had a creative and even cavalier attitude towards quoting and inter-preting Scripture. For example, Psalm 68.18 uses the image of a victory procession to describe God's receiving gifts from people. The author of Ephesians stands that image on its head and, in quoting that verse, writes that 'he gave gifts to his people' (4.7). Even so, the fatherhood of God is so central to the teaching of Jesus and developed Trinitarian theology that playing fast and loose with the Lord's Prayer could be considered to be the far side of creative and cavalier.

Anyway there are grave problems in calling God 'Creator'. I imagine myself, more than 30 years ago, introducing an undergraduate friend to my male parent for the first time: 'Ralph, this is my creator.' It would not be wrong to do this, but it would be very odd. Actually, I said 'Ralph, this is my father.' Jesus' message was that God is amazingly close to humans, so much so that it can be extravagantly and humorously claimed that every hair on our head is counted (Matthew 10.30). God did not just create us for the heck of it, but out of love and in hope; just as we cherish the desire that our human parents did. It is ironic, then, when we use prayer to distance ourselves from God when Jesus intended that we should know his close, nurturing, abiding and transforming presence.

However, the image of a mothering God is both touching and powerful. There are a few powerful maternal images in Scripture of God panting like a woman in labour (Isaiah 42.14) and of Jesus wanting to gather up the people of Jerusalem as a hen gathers her brood under her wings (Matthew 23.37). Ursula King and other scholars have urged us to extend the range of images that we use in worship and in picturing God. She has written an excellent book about Christian mystics, and her descriptions of their experiences show how widely some of them ranged in their depictions of transcendent reality, not least in rescuing maternal and other feminine images for God. Most of them, however, built upon and freed-up the religious tradition they inherited, and (though this would have been understandable) did not spend overmuch time fault-finding. They did not so much tinker with tradition as deepen its insights. God used frail and faulty words and an imperfect religious tradition to empower them and, through their wisdom, to touch our hearts and minds.

Worship is where we orient ourselves to divine reality in such a way as to be inspired by it, just as Prince Vladimir's courtiers were. We miss this capacity if it is dull and boring, or all surface and glitter, or if it excludes and alienates us. Even so, it is not about us in any attention-seeking or trivial way: it should inspire us to be good more than make us feel good. At its best, worship draws us memorably into the drama of salvation. Some Protestant worship is so wordy, and so contemptuous of colour and light and other symbols, that it misses the point that the Christian story of death and resurrection can be set forth in such a way that 'we cannot forget that beauty'. The Eucharist re-enacts before our eyes and with our own lively involvement the life and death of Jesus, and settles us in the conviction that 'dying, we live' (2 Corinthians 6.9). A good sermon, artfully delivered, can engage us, not as a passive audience but as active participants in the good news that it unfolds. Scripture lessons, skilfully read, draw us into the ways in which God has spoken to humans over the centuries, and encourage us to believe that he still speaks to those who wait upon his word.

Worship's primary purpose is not to provide correct words and ideas about God and our current insights into the human condition that we must monitor for their up-to-date respectability. Worship is meant to improve and inspire us. It judges us more than we judge it. We should remember that when we update and improve it, as, to some extent, we must.

A lamp to my feet

'Your word is a lamp to my feet and a light to my path' (Psalm 119.105). Lady Jane Grey, the tragic nine-day queen of England in 1553, was executed at the tender age of 16. In her last letter to her sister Catherine, she commended to her the reading of the Bible: 'It will teach you to live and learn you to die.'

Most Christians would agree with this poignant comment.

The difficulty comes in the 'how'. The father of the groom at a wedding I recently presided over drew me aside to tell me that he was a Bible man, and simply put into practice what it commanded. He was somewhat taken aback when I asked him if he was a polygamist like our father Abraham, and, if not, why not. My point was, of course, that he did not simply put into practice what it commanded, and that this is a good thing. The many and variant interpretations of the Bible divide Christians as much as they unite them. Behind them lies the fascinating and divisive question: wherein lies its authority?

All mainstream Christian denominations use the Bible in worship, so we are best to begin there with an understanding of its power. For most of Christian history, much of the Bible's power has been aural not oral, heard in worship rather than read in the study.[3] The earliest completed 'books' of the New Testament, Paul's letters, were meant to be read out to the Christian communities ('brothers and sisters') to which they were sent. The Gospels also were written for specific Christian groups and would have been read out to them. Jesus himself left no written accounts of his teaching, relying upon the individuals and crowds to whom he spoke to hear his word and act upon it: therein lay its power. Many primal faiths of humankind, including African Traditional or Native American Religions, have no written scripture at all,[4] though they have a longstanding oral tradition of myths and stories that tell of God and the gods and light up life's deepest meanings.

In the early times of the Christian religion, Scripture would have been read out in worship. As the New Testament gradually took shape, it joined readings of the Hebrew Bible in Christian worship. Jesus himself read words from the book of Isaiah in his local synagogue (Luke 4.16–19). In many times and places, even nowadays, the majority of people cannot read, at least not as easily as they can hear. So the Bible is an experience that comes to life in the imaginative power of people to engage with the heard word. Moreover, as people hear

Scripture read to a congregation, they can talk with their neighbours about it and pool their insights into its meaning. When individuals just read it to themselves privately, they do not have the pleasure and privilege of learning together, and of being built up as members of the body of Christ. Private reading of Scripture, like private worship, is important, but it cannot take the place of meeting and learning with others.

Imagine, for example, those first audiences who heard Luke's account of the parable of the Prodigal Son read out to them. They would have been shocked, surprised and amused by this remarkable and subversive story and, if it was spoken in the context of worship, as would often have been the case, they would naturally have assumed that God was saying something momentous to them through it: it was not just the life and times of a dysfunctional family. They must have wondered about the reactions of the various crowds to whom Jesus himself had spoken it (why would he have told such a good story only once?), and whether their reactions had been the same or different. As the story was told them again and again, they would have seen different things in it. They would have asked where they fitted into the story, and what they might have done if they were one of its characters. Of course, there have been many more audiences for this story in the two millennia since, and the different languages and cultures in which it has been told will have conjured from it different nuances of meaning, many of which Jesus and those who first passed it on, and Luke himself and the early readers of his Gospel, would not have recognized. Without question, some of these nuances could take away from the dramatic power of the story to shake us up and surprise us into new understandings of the depths of grace, but there is no reason to suppose that all of these new ideas are valueless. By choosing to tell stories, Jesus committed himself to an art form over which he did not have total control. It is a risky way to get across information about God, but he was a man who took risks.

The Bible's capacity to shake us up, disturb our prejudices and show them to us in the clear light of day, and astonish us with God's delight in us, is far more important than some of the conventional ways in which we interpret it. Instead of letting it speak to us, we often take it by the scruff of its neck, and shake meanings out of it that suit our prejudices. Some regard it as a scientific textbook. Others see it as a book of prophecies about the end times, detailing relatively precise information about what will happen, and in what order, before all temporal things give way to the life of heaven. Others use it to justify their political or patriarchal or other prejudices. One of the many problems with such anachronistic and totalitarian views of the Bible is that they turn a series of varied documents into a huge tract that privileges particular and peculiar and usually self-serving ways of reading it. It is a good rule of thumb, when reading the Bible, to take it most seriously when it is telling us something about God and about us that we do not really want to hear but which we suspect may be true.

The greatest achievement of the Protestant Reformation was arguably to insist that the Bible could and should be available for individuals to read in the vernacular. Ironically, that came at the cost of making it a document that was sometimes read more than it was read out, pored over more than it was heard. Of course it is necessary to scrutinize the Bible carefully, to apply the tools of knowledge to it. The whole Bible is now available in over 400 languages, and parts of it in many more: it is not now the preserve of those who know Latin or Hebrew or Greek. But this 'democratization' of Scripture does not mean that we should shape it to our desires and fantasies. Luther and others intended that it should reform us, and make us aware of its capacity to turn our world upside down and bring us to God.

Many fundamentalists and some other conservative groups think of themselves as Bible Christians, and condemn others for not taking Scripture with the seriousness it deserves. But in fact, they use it as a drunk uses a lamp-post, not so much for illumination as for support. The literalism to which they subject Scripture is a curious parody of the modernist tendency to think that all useful information comes in prosy and factual form, to confirm particular conclusions. Actually, the Bible is a library of books: it contains different genres of literature. In it, we find history, prophecy, biography and other subjects, told in a range of styles. Moreover, these 'subjects' are hardly dealt with in the way of modern scholars. For example, from Scripture we can put together a reasonably convincing account (with many gaps and some significant problem areas) of the lives of Moses and Jesus, but the biblical writers did not intend to write their biographies in ways we consider appropriate today. They chose their material to illustrate how God used such people to bring about his purpose, which was not, for example, the rationale of the writers whose biography of Mao Tse-Tung I have recently finished (still less the desire of Mao himself). It is foolish to condemn the biblical writers for failing to follow our current academic guidelines or assumptions.

Or for not noticing that they fail to follow our religious guidelines: their concerns were not always ours, and we would do well to try to understand rather than second-guess them. Those 'Bible Christians' who pore over Scripture to read their own paranoia into it miss this obvious point. Many of them think that the Hebrew prophets' primary function was to predict future events. Yet they were more intent upon telling their contemporaries what the result of breaking the covenant with God would be (usually mayhem and destruction) than in predicting the future like some modern-day astrologist writing for a newspaper. They read the signs of the times, not tea-leaves at the bottom of a gullible person's cup. We Christians (and even our earliest ancestors in the faith who wrote the works of the New Testament) may wrest a prediction of the coming of Jesus out of Isaiah, and Micah, and other prophets; but they were too busy telling their contemporaries what would be the results of present disobedience to waste their time overmuch in describing the far-away future. They told forth the wrath and the grace of God more than they foretold its long-term outcomes. Like any enduring work of art and literature, their sayings accrued new meanings and interpretations as time went by, in the reading of future generations. Even so, such readings, to make sense, need to be the result of the creative and controlled and not the diseased imagination. The authors of the books of Daniel and Revelation, writing in the apocalyptic genre, are more along the lines of prophets as we have come to interpret prophets, but their deliberately arcane and symbolic use of language means that twenty-first-century readers have little purchase on how to divine what they originally meant to convey. When Christians interpret their poetic and elusive flights with often hateful and always prosy literalism, they are doomed to disappointment, and deserve to be rebuked for their wasteful enterprise that sometimes has wicked consequences.

In the USA, such 'Bible Christians' often get away with claiming that they alone are Christians. They should not be allowed to, and it is a pleasure to read other conservative Christian writers standing up to them. For their silly and sometimes wicked readings of Scripture privilege views that make it very difficult to enact programmes to care for the world's resources or to create and sustain peace in the Middle East: many such Christians see the world's end at hand so cannot be bothered to look after it; and they support the return of many Jews to Israel, not out of any love or respect for Jews or their faith, but to hasten the end times which, they believe, require a large Jewish population in Zion.

Such literal readings of Scripture are often assumed to be the only way to read it, not just by 'Bible Christians' but by critics of Christianity such as (among the writers we have referred to) Sam Harris, Christopher Hitchens and Richard Dawkins. A small amount of research and thought would reveal the oddness of this position. If a library contains a variety of books, it needs a variety of different strategies to read and understand it: you would not expect to read a story about someone like Moses in the same way that you would read a paean of praise to God or a symbolic uncovering of the future of a world cared for by God.

In fact, for many centuries the most common way of reading Scripture was allegorical, and its weaknesses (it also had some significant strengths) can be seen in St Augustine's interpretation of the parable of the Good Samaritan. He gives everything in the story a fixed, allegorical explanation: the man set on by thieves is Adam; Jerusalem is the heavenly city from which we have been exiled; Jericho is the moon, symbolizing our death, for it rises and decays; the Samaritan is Jesus; the inn is the Church; and so forth. It is a fascinating read but Augustine sucks the life out of the story by robbing it of the power to change us. He makes us know the story's meaning in detail whereas, however well we are familiar with it, it should retain at every hearing or reading the capacity to surprise and renew us, not just edify us.

Augustine tells the parable in more than one of his writings. In his *Quaestiones Evangeliorum*, it serves to illustrate church doctrine, at least as he and many western fathers of the Church understood it. The Bible has become the servant of the Church. To a point, this is a simple matter of fact, though not one that some Protestants want to hear. Many Protestants underplay, or deny, or simply do not know, the fact that the Bible is the creation of the Church, part of the developing Christian tradition of faith. In his Easter Letter of 367, Bishop Athanasius of Alexandria listed the books of what would become the New Testament, and used the word 'canon' (rule: regulator of Christian life) of them. Thereafter, the Bible began to be accepted in its present shape. Yet it had taken a while, and several local and Ecumenical Councils, for the Christian Bible to emerge in its present form, and there are still differences of opinion between, on the one hand, Catholics and Orthodox, and, on the other, Protestants, about whether some books should be included or not. Some evangelical Christians try to avoid seeing the Bible as the creation of the Church by arguing that Paul (2 Timothy 4.11–13), Peter (2 Peter 3.15–16) and John (Revelation 22.18–19) fixed the canon of the New Testament, but this requires an unconvincing and doctrinaire reworking of history that would convince no thoughtful person but one who is determined that it should.

To make this point is not to support Augustine's interpretation of the parable of the Good Samaritan, still less to suggest that the Church, in certain of its forms, has sole rights to interpret Scripture to its own advantage. The whole Church owes a debt to Luther and other reformers for letting the Bible speak afresh and powerfully, so that it is not forced to become the servant of any particular group. Ironically, many self-designated 'Bible Christians' handle it with just the same confidence, narrowness and cluelessness as did those whom the reformers condemned. In emphasizing that the important role given to the Bible, and what are its constituent parts, is the creation of the Church, our point is that we should avoid making an idol out of it. It is of central importance to the Church, but it does not replace the Church and its accumulated wisdom, which it has helped to shape; it contains all things necessary for salvation, but it is not God, who alone saves fallen humans.

The Bible records a small but astonishingly meaningful part of the record of God's dealings with his human children. It tells us of God's love, and our human capacity to respond to that love. It tells the story of Israel and of Jesus. It is not only Jews and Christians who are the recipients of God's grace: 'Did I not bring Israel up from the land of Egypt, and the Philistines from Caphtor and the Arameans from Kir?' (Amos 9.7). Nor are they alone able to respond to God's grace, for among all the peoples of the earth there are those who inherit the kingdom, having seen Jesus in the guise of the hungry, thirsty, stranger, naked, sick and imprisoned (Matthew 25.31–46). Yet Christians believe that Jesus is the human face of God, and that the Bible describes the nature and actions of this Christ-like God, who speaks to us in order that we follow and become like him. Without the Bible we would not know this. But it is a means, not the end. Most Christians have not been persuaded of the Muslim conviction that Scripture is the precise word of God in all its details, though they recognize that the Bible does contain words from God and points to the incarnate word of God, Jesus himself (John 1.14).

The biblical words come to us through human agencies, fallible men and women who were nevertheless hungry for God and inspired by him. The Bible does not try to play down the imperfection and shortcomings of humans to whom God spoke and whom he used in his purposes. Abraham, Jacob, Samuel, David, Peter, Paul, John Mark and many other biblical heroes have feet of clay. This is not just our twenty-first-century take. The original stories tell their stories, warts and all. Even the developing sense in the early Church that Jesus was the perfect man[5] should not blind us to the fact of his capacity for growth in human perception and understanding. For example, even he, who specialized in surprising people, was himself surprised by the astonishing faith of a Roman soldier (Matthew 8.5–13) and a Canaanite woman (Matthew 15.21–28).

Except among noisy but eccentric groups, Christians are not committed to the belief that the Scripture is faultless. They do not and should not resort to the notion that God dictated it, so that whatever it says, contradictions and all, has to be contorted into a single unconvincing interpretation. It is the very fallibility of the Bible that permitted Martin Luther to call the letter of James 'a right strawy epistle'. Many people have followed Luther in favouring some parts of Scripture over others. Sometimes these preferences show our own questionable assumptions, which can, however, be intriguing and even revolutionary (Luther much preferred Paul to James, and read Paul to privilege justification by faith, which not all scholars have done and which James was sceptical about:[6] nevertheless, for good and ill, Paul turned the Church upside down). Sometimes, however, these preferences show a measure of mature judgement and common sense: some parts of Scripture are self-evidently more edifying than others. Given the propensity of many Christians to blunder about in the book of Revelation, it becomes easier to admit and admire the wisdom of those fathers of the Church, especially in the East, who were doubtful about the value of including it in the New Testament canon.

There was a tendency, a generation or two ago, among some liberal Christians to place the Bible alongside the works of Shakespeare, Tolstoy and other great compositions as one of humankind's great literary treasures. There was also a move in some interfaith circles to corral the Bible with the Qur'an, the Bhagavad Gita, the Tao Te Ching and other scriptures as priceless religious writings. It is no disrespect to these other august works to maintain that such were false moves.

To understand the particular importance of the Bible for Christian life, we should return to the profoundly religious concept that there is a depth to life that Christians call God, who speaks to us and calls forth our faith, hope and love. Like many other people of faith, Christians respond to that vocation. The Bible provides a record of such divine and human encounter. Since humans are necessarily limited by time and space, as well as prone to mistakes and to sin, it is not likely, indeed not possible, that the Bible is a perfect production. It records the human quest for God as it is, not in some idealized way. It inspired its writers and inspires us to give our lives to God.

Christians should disagree with those of their number who eccentrically and unconvincingly ascribe sole authorship of the biblical production to God. They also differ from Muslims and those other people of faith who see their scripture in this way. As eastern Christians, and John Wesley and his Methodist people (among others), have long known, we are imperfect human beings who, through a relationship with God, grow into holiness. The quest for truth depends upon the view, not that

Scripture is an inerrant guide, but rather that it shows us why and how others have made a similar journey to ours. Scripture is not a tick list to be checked off before God is pleased with and accepting of us. Nor is it a scientific manual, a handbook for the end of days, an ethical scold that motivates us by making us feel guilty and disempowered, or a million and one other things that the sublimely uninspired have made it to be. Of course there is material in it about the glories of nature, the future hope of humans and the created order, the good life, and many other things, though rarely in so simplistic a way as some narrow-minded devotees believe. It has been called, with much justification, The Book of God.

Living in faith and hope

Christians have the grounding of Scripture and the resources of worship from which to develop their relationship with the living God, whose love is greater than we can imagine and more patient than we deserve. They also have the treasures of Christian history from which to draw, creatively and with discernment.

The bond we have with God grows and develops with the years. This is bound to mean that our understanding of what God wants of us similarly changes and, hopefully, deepens. A grave mistake that Christians and many other people of faith make is to assert or assume that God has placed us in a world where there are straightforward answers to difficult issues, and that these answers are the same for all people, at all times, everywhere. We can see this in attitudes to the environment, abortion, and many, many other decisions that face people in contemporary times. More often than not, there are no easy answers, and people of faith who maintain that there are usually have axes that others can hear, grinding noisily. It is, for example, difficult to take seriously those men who consider abortion to be an unforgivable sin because a foetus is a living human being, yet who unthinkingly support the death penalty, foreign invasions and other instruments of death. It is reasonable to suppose that their real desire is to assert the right of men to tell women what they can and cannot do with their lives and their bodies, and to associate God with that viewpoint. They do not do God's will; he is made to do theirs, and is used to defend and excuse their bigotry. No doubt many such people believe their own deception. As the prophet Jeremiah put it (17.9), 'The heart is devious above all else; it is perverse – who can understand it?' That such perversion is strongly believed does not excuse it: bigotry is bigotry, however sincerely believed. However, to identify and spell out such manipulation does not mean that abortion is a virtuous act, or answer the question of when life begins, or assume that men can have no say in the issues around abortion, or resolve a cluster of other issues. Complex issues demand careful reasoning, and a great deal of faith, hope and love.

With the resources we have, the Christian vocation is to seek to determine how faithfully to obey God in the world in which we are placed, which is not the world of Moses, nor even of Jesus and Paul. It is daft to pretend that we do not know what the natural and human sciences have taught us, and unfaithful to ignore their insights, though we should test them for their credibility and usefulness.

As examples of how to proceed, let us revisit two issues we have already raised: violence and homosexuality.

The involvement of religion in violence was, as we have seen, a contributory factor to its marginalization in Enlightenment and post-Enlightenment Europe. Nowadays, many critics of religion pick on the Pats and Osamas of this world in order to deem it a phenomenon whose days on earth should be numbered, if we wish there to be more days on earth. They forget, ignore or do not know of the many religious peace groups around the world. Nor do they recognize that many iconic religious figures of the last hundred years have been motivated by religion's teachings of a peaceable kingdom in which all can flourish, and work to bring about its foretaste in their time on earth: Mahatma Gandhi, Martin Luther King, Nelson Mandela, Desmond Tutu and others. Christians are followers of the Prince of Peace, who nevertheless warned that his message could divide families and wider groups (Mark 13.9–13): appallingly, it is so much easier to love the few than the many, and to make God a tribal rather than a universal deity. So, although there is a long and honourable Christian tradition of pacifism, many more Christians recognize that it is necessary to stand up and fight tyranny and injustice, even, if necessary, with real weapons, not just with the weapon of words.

If it is true that the modern world has given religions tighter boundaries than was formerly the case, then it is possible and sensible to argue, against those who blame religion for every evil thing, that it is not just bad faith that causes and justifies needless violence. Faith was used in medieval Europe to validate the crusades and other wars, but other dimensions in society, especially politics and economics, were contributory factors: kings and emperors wanted glory and money, and landless soldiers wanted to find some place of their own or else some other booty. This does not get religion off the hook, but it does mean that simplistic notions of religion spoiling everything are quite absurd: if bad faith were replaced by no faith, there would be political, economic and other justifications for evil deeds. And the one dimension that gives a profound analysis of the evil that haunts humankind would have been removed. For the secularism that produced Stalin, Hitler, Mao and Pol Pot has no significant explanation to offer for the shortcomings of humanity.

Aggression between different religious communities (often intra- rather than inter-faith) arises out of a mistaken notion of the point of religion, whether as a dimension in life or a bound-aried phenomenon. Religions are not true, though they can and should point to the truth: God in relationship with us. To fight for Christianity, or its European expressions, or for Islam, or Sunni rather than Shia faith, is usually an act of folly and wickedness, be it held with ever such fervour and honesty: enthusiasm and integrity in default of insight and wisdom are not the absolute virtues some people claim them to be. In his rather special little book on *The Bible as Prayer*, the distinguished British concert pianist Stephen Hough, a gay man and convert to Roman Catholicism, makes a point about the Old Testament that could be applied *mutatis mutandis* to many other scriptures and faith traditions: 'the Old Testament contains one of the great learning curves in literature – the story of a people's gradual, humbling discovery that God is not part of the endless cycle of violence which our human frenzy projects on to him'.[7]

The glory of any religion is not when it defends itself and puts limits on who can join the saved: it is when it tells of God, who is like a father who loves his children to excess, even when they wish he were dead. Muslim suicide bombers, Jewish settlers who assume a divine right to land at the expense of others, Christians who harass and even murder doctors in abortion clinics: these and other such religious people are not interested in the living God so much as in turning religion into a haven for and justification of their vicious deeds and exclusive fantasies by claiming or just assuming, dementedly and wickedly, that they have his sanction. Religious people should be able to agree that violence is a last resort, not to defend God (who can look after himself) or a particular expression of religious life and belief, but to combat that extreme darkness that has no place for love and its desire to grace and nurture all people.

Other agreements are not so easy to define as many partisan proponents of defined positions assert. There is, for example, no one right solution to enable peace in the Middle East. Rather, today's complex and tragic situation is the result of a long history of shocking violence, admirable co-existence, and outside interference. Those who look to Scripture or elsewhere for the right answer or answers usually read into it a prejudice rather than out of it an inspired solution. We have to look within, not outside, ourselves, to locate the empowering Spirit of God, to recognize her desire for an inclusive and compassionate solution to the dilemmas caused by human sin, and our own imperfections and shortcomings. Since holiness is a lifelong quest, not an instant given, we should mostly be willing to compromise rather than to insist on our point of view. Life is not so much a series of right answers as a capacity to muddle through, with the help of God's grace that entices us to search after his rightness and righteousness, not our own.

My nearby city of Chicago has recently put on a Silk Road exhibition, not only in the Art Museum but also in concerts in Symphony Hall. To see clothes or art or even furniture, or to hear 'fusion music', that were the result of East meeting West on the trade routes between Europe and China is to realize that inter-cultural encounter has not always been violent. It has sometimes been mutually beneficial, and even friendly. And this has been true, also, of relations between religions. Those who think that some religions and cultures (never their own, but always someone else's) are intrinsically violent may be saying more about their own deepest and uninformed fears than the truth of things.

Given the perilous state of the world, one would hope and suppose that the Church (and all religions) would have much to say about injustice, global warming, famine, holocausts and other disasters, actual and potential. Instead, many Christians are more concerned with a range of issues to do with the human body. A number of Anglican archbishops are among many contemporary Christians who apparently think that homosexuality is a sin much greater than poverty, abuse of the environment and other pressing issues that threaten the stability and future of our fragile planet. Some of these are from Africa, so this is the place to question the assumption of many people that the future of world Christianity lies there and in other non-western lands, where conservatism dominates. It may well lie there, as recent books by Philip Jenkins suggest, but his view of what this will entail could prove him to be a false prophet. As it happens, some African church leaders are appalled by the rigid and irrelevant social conservatism, theological ineptness and personal grandiosity of some of their colleagues, and say so loudly.[8] It will be interesting to watch events unfold there.

Many outsiders are puzzled by the obsession of some noisy Christians with human sexuality. For it is an obsession: there are very few references to homosexuality in Scripture. Indeed, given that the Bible knows nothing of modern analyses of nature, nurture, desire and psycho-sexual integration, one could claim that it does not refer to homosexuality at all, and that all its views about human (not just homo-) sexuality reflect a premodern worldview that is largely alien to us. Jesus himself was notably silent on the issue on homosexuality, except for one interesting story to which we shall shortly turn. It will not quite do to argue that he would have accepted the Jewish teaching of his day about monogamous marriage: he was stricter about divorce than many Jewish teachers of his day and many Southern Baptists of ours, at least in Mark 10.1–12 where he allows for no divorce at all. Moreover, he did not see marriage and a family as quite the ideal that most of his co-religionists did, for although, in that Marcan passage, he quoted from his scripture to justify marriage as the union of one man and one woman, his own marital status is unclear and he put loyalty to his vision of God's kingdom above ordinary family commitments. We should also bear in mind that the family as Jesus knew it would not have been that of the western nuclear family, with generations separated into different dwellings and living in different places. If we wish to shore up biblical standards of marriage, we have to ask which ones: neither the polygamy of the patriarchs nor Paul's encouragement to the single state and celibacy would have many Christian takers today. In fact, we do not live in any of the Bible's worlds, so our calling is to work out, in the power of God's abiding Spirit, what are appropriate life-enhancing relationships that can sustain people and make them holy in today's varied societies.

There are several worlds of the Bible. In them, people mostly had arranged marriages and produced children in order for the group to survive and to pass scarce land down through the family line. Many husbands and wives would have fallen in love after they were married and people of all cultures love their children but, until our own day, in most societies many women died in childhood and lots of children were carried off by disease before they grew up. We cannot draw easy parallels between our own views of marriage, whether Nigerian, Australian, English or North American, and those of Jews in the ancient world.

In parts of the contemporary world, over-population is a problem, whereas in many parts of the ancient world replenishing the population in contexts of terrible disease and occasional wars was more likely to be an anxiety. Exclusively same-sex relations and sometimes even masturbation would then be seen as a social evil, at times when the population needed to be maintained at a reasonable level. Moreover, although our modern understandings of homosexuality are still developing, it is clear enough that for many contemporary people human sexuality seems no more a choice than the colour of their skin or their place of birth: we are what we are.

Many heterosexual people view the thought of homosexual activity with repugnance and fear. People have sometimes responded that way to those of a different colour and from a different culture to themselves, and have needed to understand the roots of such phobias and get over them. Once they have done so, they have not only seen our common humanity but have even learned from differences about the various ways of being human.

One passage that is sometimes used to suggest that Jesus overlooked homosexual practice is the story of the healing of the centurion's servant (Matthew 8.5–13; Luke 7.1–10). The soldier was obviously devoted to his servant because, instead of following the usual practice of replacing a dying slave with a living one, he requested Jesus to heal him. The assumption of some scholars is that this socially unequal relationship of genuine affection, at least on the part of the centurion, would have been sexually expressed, because the soldier had the power to make it so even if the young man did not want his attentions. It is reasonable to interpret the story in this way, for many soldiers billeted abroad among a hostile population would have taken pleasure wherever they could find it, and a pretty boy would sometimes suffice. It was rumoured that Roman soldiers behaved in this way, and Jesus would no doubt have heard such gossip. That he healed the centurion's servant suggests that he condoned such behaviour even if he did not approve it. Except: we have no way of knowing if this possibility of a homosexual relationship between the officer and his slave was actually the case in this story, which emphasizes Jesus' admiration of the soldier's faith in his authority to heal, not the centurion's personal morality or lifestyle. Still, it is a tantalizing story and, since shrill opponents of homosexuality make much out of little biblical evidence, they can hardly complain if others follow their lead to make a different case.

We are on safer ground in using the miracle of the healing of the centurion's servant to make a different but relevant point. Jesus was prepared to do the bidding of an agent of foreign oppression, not out of fear but out of respect for him. Rarely does Jesus conform to the ethical and social values that we would like him to: many Jews hated Roman rule because they believed that God was their only ruler, and it is easy to assume that Jesus would have believed the same and so shunned foreign soldiers. Up to a point, he probably did. Yet he was a man who could see goodness or the potential for it in collaborators, whores, children and foreigners. He was interested in people who knew their need of God, even if they were despised, disempowered, shunned or marginalized by most people and by conventional morality. So to make Jesus strongly intolerant of homosexual practices is as misguided, stupid even, as to make him a strong advocate of them. One can assume that God's Spirit is as unimpressed by certain aspects of our own conventional morality as Jesus was of his, and looks beyond them to signs of people in need, who look for grace and who may not find it from sanctimonious church leaders and many other Christians.

Different ages have particular issues to deal with, and have to see them afresh in the light, not of unchanging biblical rules, but of the law of love that our relationship with God demands we live.

Is our negative attitude towards homosexuality a proper response to sin, or is it more like Christian attitudes towards slavery? Jefferson Davis, President of the Confederate States during the American Civil War of 1861–5, wrote that:

> [slavery] was established by decree of Almighty God . . . it is sanctioned in the Bible, in both Testaments, from Genesis to Revelation . . . it has existed in all ages, has been found among the people of the highest civilization, and in nations of the highest proficiency in the arts.

He had a point. It was a part of the Old Testament world. Jesus said nothing directly about slavery. Paul accepted it as part of the fabric of society, even, as the short letter to Philemon makes plain, sending a runaway slave back to his master, a friend of Paul's, with the appeal that he would 'welcome him as you would welcome me' (verse 17), though Philemon could have branded or even killed him. Since the letter survives, presumably so did Onesimus, the slave – in all probability, still as a slave.

It took centuries for Christians to admit that slavery is always wrong, and longer to right it. This has also been true in Islam,

Hinduism and other religions. Contemporary religious people who look for specific guidance to the Bible or the Qur'an or some other scripture or hallowed documents simply factor out the acceptance of slavery to be found there. Or else they point to passages that provide the justification for a process that would eventually lead, centuries later, to its abolition. For example, if Paul could return a slave to his owner, thereby risking his death, he could also write: 'There is no longer Jew or Greek, there is no longer slave or free, there is no longer male and female; for all of you are one in Christ Jesus' (Galatians 3.28). If it is the case that our understanding of human dignity has changed to the point where we can hardly believe that people accepted slavery for centuries, often unquestioningly, we should be open to the possibility that we too have our blind spots. Indeed, it is only within the last half-century that centuries of anti-Semitism have been challenged and overcome in the teachings of Christian churches. If the condemnation and marginalization of gay people is a comparable folly, then those who perpetrate this prejudice will rightly be regarded by generations to come as scandalously slow to see their bigotry for what it is.

In all these cases, we are dealing with real people. When we use the Bible in the way that Jefferson Davis did to justify slavery, or Christians like Luther did to attack Jews, or in the way some Christians do to condemn gay people, we prefer rules to people. This was hardly the reaction of Jesus, who observed that 'the Sabbath was made for men and women, not men and women for the Sabbath' (Mark 2.27).[9]

The purpose of raising these currently contentious issues of religion's role in violence and its attitude towards homosexuality is not to provide right answers to replace a present range of bad answers; though some answers, however widely held, are clearly bad in the way in which they have been reached and in their consequences for God's children. Rather, it is to urge us to locate our Christian vocation in a living and developing relationship with God, grounded in Scripture, sustained in worship and drawing faithfully and discerningly from tradition. Our calling is not to use the Bible or tradition as rule-books, for the simple reason that we are not tenth-century BCE Jews or first-century Christians or fifteenth-century Venetians, or . . . well, you get the point. Yet, because God speaks to people in and through the Bible and in and through Christian history, and because the stories of Jesus begin in Scripture and inspire all Christians since, the Bible and tradition are of inestimable value in shaping the way in which we are faithful to God in our own day and setting.

A necessary end

Cowards die many times before their deaths;
The valiant never taste of death but once.
Of all the wonders that I yet have heard,
It seems to me most strange that men should fear;
Seeing that death, a necessary end,
Will come when it will come.

So says Shakespeare's Julius Caesar. For many sceptics, people are misguidedly religious out of a strange fear of death and an unwillingness to contemplate their eternal extinction. Such cynicism cannot bear close scrutiny. Lots of people fear death but religions do not always or even usually offer false and sentimental comforts. Some religions, such as Judaism, have been vague about life after death, and many Jews still express hesitancy about the life of the world to come. Certainly, for most of the Old Testament period Jews had no belief in individual survival: God's breath returned to him at death, and any survival was in Sheol, a place where righteous and unrighteous alike had a gloomy, twilight existence. People of the Old Testament believed that the goodness of God was to be encountered in the land of the living, not in the abode of the dead. By the beginning of the Common Era, many but not all Jews had come to believe in the resurrection of the chosen people or even of individuals. No doubt this belief grew up against the background of the deaths of Jews in their successful revolt against Hellenistic occupation in the second century BCE. But this was not the only factor. Some Old Testament writers wrote movingly of a relationship with God of such force and meaning that it seemed as if only death could destroy it: 'Turn, O LORD, save my life; deliver me for the sake of your steadfast love. For in death there is no remembrance of you; in Sheol who can give you praise?' (Psalm 6.4–5) It was but a short move to believe that not even death can destroy a relationship with God, a view that Jesus accepted and passed on to early Christians who identified being with Jesus as part of that ongoing, deathless relationship (Romans 8.38–39).

Aeons before Jesus, Neanderthal people used red ochre to stain bones in burial grounds. We can only guess why, but it is reasonable to suppose that they were expressing great awe before the mystery of death. It is that sense of mystery which this book has attempted to indicate and tease out. It is an innate instinct of most humans to respond in wonder to life's mysteries, the greatest of which is not death, but the meaning of life, which death closes off and makes us ponder. There is a significant weight of evidence that humans can respond to a transcendent dimension to life and that, when they do, this can transform their lives in faith and hope and love.

What does this mean about death? People have many ideas of what lies beyond death. Some picture it somewhat like a family reunion at an airport lounge. Others want to meet and talk with Jesus or a favoured figure from the past. Others want wrongs righted or wounds healed. And so on. We are driven to use the language of hope and of symbol, some expressions of which will speak more meaningfully to one group than another. St Paul wrote:

'What no eye has seen, nor ear heard, nor the human heart conceived, what God has prepared for those who love him' – these things God has revealed to us through the Spirit; for the Spirit searches everything, even the depths of God. (1 Corinthians 2.9–10)

In other words, through our relationship with God we learn the wonders of his deathless love for us. Not only that, our own love reaches its fulfilment. As Charles Wesley put it in one of his greatest hymns:

Spirit of Holiness, let all Thy saints adore
Thy sacred energy, and bless Thine heart renewing power.
Not angel tongues can tell Thy love's ecstatic height,
The glorious joy unspeakable the beatific sight.

Eternal, Triune God, let all the hosts above,
Let all on earth below record and dwell upon Thy love.
When heaven and earth are fled before Thy glorious face,
Sing all the saints Thy love hath made Thine everlasting
    praise.

This is not the happy ending of a fairy tale, but the culmination of the story of God's initiative to seek and save the lost. Paul could picture death as the last enemy, for sin and selfishness can draw humans away from the source of life. Yet in the same moment that he names that enemy, he also tells us that God will destroy death (1 Corinthians 15.26). So death can be greeted as a friend, as in these words attributed to Francis of Assisi:

And thou, most kind and gentle death,
waiting to hush our latest breath,
O praise him, alleluia.
Thou leadest home the child of God,
and Christ our Lord the way hath trod.

Nobody knows what precisely death will bring. Religion gives us hope, not knowledge. It is life's last great adventure. Just as one cannot tell where a close relationship with a spouse, partner or friend will lead us in the years to come, though one can hope that it will broaden and deepen to give great happiness and contentment, so one trusts that the relationship we have with God will confer limitless fulfilment and meaning.

That relationship has been the subject of much modern and postmodern speculation, as this book has illustrated. Some think that religion is not about God at all, and that any attempt to enter into a relationship with her is as doomed to failure as attempting to befriend or marry the tooth fairy. Others depict God in such a way that many sensitive souls would wish to steer clear of him, who desires not so much a relationship as rigid conformity to often outlandish and outdated rules and who judges humans not out of love but out of ten for their knowledge of and obedience to his arbitrary demands.

It is the contention of this book that humans should live as if God loves them, completely and for always. The truth of this contention can be found in giving our heart and mind and soul to it. When we do, we discover, as we can bear it, the nature and the name of love.

Notes

Introduction and Acknowledgements

1 Mark Twain so referred to the Book of Mormon.
2 I have substituted the translation 'stranger' for the NRSV's 'alien'.

Chapter 1

1 Modernist interpretations of religion are described in chapter 2.
2 See, for example, the book on Islam and science by Seyyid Hossein Nasr, included in the bibliography.
3 This quotation is part of the subtitle of a book by Christopher Hitchens, included in the bibliography.
4 Walter Isaacson, *Einstein: His Life and Universe*, New York, Simon & Schuster, 2007, p. 389.
5 Richard Dawkins, *The God Delusion*, London, Bantam Press, 2006, p. 50.
6 Dawkins, *God Delusion*, p. 1.
7 Christopher Hitchens, *God is Not Great: How Religion Poisons Everything*, New York and Boston, Twelve, 2007, p. 230.
8 As I write these words in May 2007, there is much debate in the media about the linkage between right-wing religion and the Republican Party, whether the influence is good, and if it is waning. More interesting are the growing number of 'Bible-believing' evangelicals who are questioning the link, and who are extending the repertoire of their religious rhetoric to include a positive take on environmental and other issues.
9 Hanna Rosin, *God's Harvard: A Christian College on a Mission to Save America*, Orlando, Harcourt, 2007, p.8.
10 Isaacson, *Einstein*, p. 389.
11 Isaacson, *Einstein*, p. 390.
12 Isaacson, *Einstein*, p. 387.
13 John Drane, *What is the New Age Saying to the Church?*, Grand Rapids, Zondervan, 1991, pp. 40, 45.

14 For an elaboration of this claim, read Michael York, *Pagan Theology: Paganism as a World Religion*, New York, New York University Press, 2003.

15 http://www.unhcr.org/basics.html.

16 Kenneth Cracknell, ed., *Wilfred Cantwell Smith: A Reader*. Oxford, Oneworld, pp. 6f.

17 http://www.cair-net.org/.

18 I take a particular pride in the work of the Leicester Council of Faiths, which I helped found in 1986, though it took the previous two years to get it off the ground: http://www.leicestercounciloffaiths.org.uk/history.html.

19 We shall look at the nature and the name of God's love later in the book.

20 This can be accessed at: http://www.jcrelations.net/en/?item=2552.

21 http://news.bbc.co.uk/2/hi/europe/6639643.stm.

Chapter 2

1 Tearfund is The Evangelical Alliance Relief Fund, and its report of April 2007 can be accessed at: http://www.tearfund.org/webdocs/Website/News/Final%20churchgoing%20report.pdf.

2 *Hymns & Psalms* 101.

3 http://www.religioustolerance.org/rel_rate.htm.

4 There are many accounts of Pope Urban II's speech and of the capture of Jerusalem by the crusaders. I have given one version of these events. Common to all accounts is the speech's invitation to violent action in the name of Christ, and the willingness of many people to take it seriously.

5 The full text can be seen at: http://www.fordham.edu/halsall/source/1204innocent.html.

6 Two recent scholars disagree about the dating of this sermon. Albert Outler dates this to 6 May 1781, and Timothy Smith much earlier to 1 October 1758. The sermon itself can be accessed at: http://wesley.nnu.edu/john_wesley/sermons/chron.htm.

7 I have written a short summary of similar Jewish views about Jesus, including those of Klausner and Vermes, in Martin Forward, *Jesus: A Short Biography*, Oxford, Oneworld, 1998, pp. 114–19.

8 Wilfred Cantwell Smith, *The Meaning and End of Religion*, London, SCM, 1978, p. 51.

9 Alfred C. Haddon, *History of Anthropology*, London and New York, The Knickerbocker Press, 1910, p. 79.

10 John Lewis Gaddis, *The Landscape of History: How Historians*

Map the Past, Oxford and New York, Oxford University Press, 2002, pp. 53f.

11 Gaddis, *Landscape*, p. 92.

12 Gaddis, *Landscape*, p. 44.

Chapter 3

1 Klaus Klostermaier, *Hindu and Christian in Vrindaban*, London, SCM, 1969, p. 84.

2 Ninian Smart, *The World's Religions*, Cambridge, Cambridge University Press, 1998, pp. 11–22.

3 Frank Whaling, *Christian Theology and World Religions: A Global Approach*, London, Marshall, Morgan & Scott, 1986, p. 38.

4 Maeonides is Homer, to whom the epic Greek poems *Iliad* and *Odyssey* are attributed.

5 Diana McVeagh, *Gerald Finzi: His Life and Music*, Woodbridge, Boydell, 2005, p. 264.

Chapter 4

1 Paulos Mar Gregorios, *A Light Too Bright: The Enlightenment Today*, New York, SUNY, p. 236.

2 E.g., The King James or Authorized Version of the Bible records, in Matthew 1.25, that Joseph 'knew her [Mary] not till she had brought forth her firstborn son: and he called his name Jesus'. It means that Joseph and Mary did not have sexual intercourse during that time. The Greek word there is γίνωσκεν, which is part of the verb 'to know'. The NRSV somewhat decorously translates (or, rather, paraphrases) it as 'had no marital relations'.

3 I have summarized the account of the origins of Muhammad's prophetic vocation that is most widely agreed among Muslims.

4 A Sufi is an Islamic mystic. There has been much debate about the origins of the word. The most commonly agreed solution is that it comes from the Arabic word for wool, referring to the garments of early Muslim ascetics.

5 This is a clearer translation than the NRSV's: '. . . Father, hallowed be your name'.

6 The allusion here is to Isaiah 57.15.

7 This comes from Sermon 24, 'Upon Our Lord's Sermon on the Mount, 4'.

8 A member of a hereditary priestly class among the ancient Medes and Persians, who later became Zoroastrians. They were often interested in astrology, as Matthew's account (2.1–12) of the visit of the magi

to the young Jesus indicated. In the quotation in the text, the term is probably used in a more general sense to indicate those who dabbled in astrology, an unislamic practice, rather than astronomy, which is permitted to Muslims.

Chapter 5

1 She spoke these words in an interview with London Weekend Television in January 1980, though she had used the idea as far back as October 1968, in a Conservative Political Centre lecture in Blackpool.

2 http://www.vatican.va/roman_curia/congregations/cfaith/documents/rc_con_cfaith_doc_20000806_dominus-iesus_en.html.

3 http://www.jcrelations.net/en/?item=2015.

4 John Hick, *An Autobiography*, Oxford, Oneworld, 2002, is an engaging summary of how this important philosopher interprets his life. Chapter 20 is particularly illuminating and gives a flavour of the exuberant self-confidence with which he holds his opinions.

5 John Hick, *God and the Universe of Faiths: Essays in the Philosophy of Religion*, Oxford, Oneworld, 1994 revised edition. The first edition dates back as far as 1973.

6 This threefold division originated in Alan Race's *Christians and Religious Pluralism: Patterns in the Christian Theology of Religions*, London, SCM, 1993 revised edition (the first edition dates to 1983).

7 http://en.fgulen.com/a.page/books/a1718.html.

8 See the introductory remarks by Kenneth Cracknell in his edited reader of some of Smith's works, and also Smith's own works to which he refers, in *Wilfred Cantwell Smith: A Reader*, Oxford, Oneworld, 2001, pp. 20ff.

9 The hyper-Calvinism of the time developed Calvin's thought, and can be found in, for example, the Westminster Confession of 1647, with which Wesley was well acquainted.

10 Albert Outler (ed.), *The Works of John Wesley*, vol. 3, Nashville, Abingdon Press, 1986, pp. 544–63.

11 Outler, *Works of John Wesley*, pp. 491–501.

12 Daniel Defoe, who went to school with Wesley's father, based his eponymous hero Robinson Crusoe upon Ibn Tufayl's creation.

13 There is, for example, a Jewish atheist web site: http://www.kofersite.com/.

14 http://www.sofn.org.uk/.

15 The Angel's words to the Soul in Cardinal Newman's *The Dream of Gerontius*.

16 'Burnt Norton'.

Notes

Chapter 6

1 Timothy Ware, *The Orthodox Church*, Harmondsworth, Penguin, 1993, p. 264.

2 '. . . there was with the angel a multitude of the heavenly host, praising God and saying . . .': Luke 2.13.

3 This is true of other scriptures also. The Islamic scripture is the Qur'an, which means 'that which is read out or uttered forth'.

4 The word 'scripture' means the act or product of writing, deriving from the Late Latin word *scriptura*.

5 In Mark 10.18, Jesus asks of the rich young man, 'Why do you call me good? No one is good but God alone.' In Matthew 19.17, Jesus says, 'Why do you ask me about what is good? There is only one who is good.' Matthew may be embarrassed by Mark's more straightforward comment, or this may simply be an example of his Jewish habit of paraphrasing references to the divine name. Those who think that Jesus was trying to get the man to admit that he was God misread the passage by placing the emphasis where it does not lie: the man goes away grieving, not because he has an inadequate view of Jesus but because his money gets in the way of his ideals. Jesus did not claim to be good. Hardly any good person does: a person's worth and stature are best assessed by others, which is one reason to be suspicious of contemporary people who claim to be spiritual.

6 Many Christian writers and preachers try to explain that there is no real difference between James and Paul, since Paul also believed that faith should issue in good works. They should lighten up a little and allow for some genuine differences between the two writers rather than manufacture an uneasy agreement between them. The pietistic tendency to make all of Scripture's voices speak with a single voice is doomed to failure, and disables us from having a conversation with them so as to work out how we can be faithful in our day and setting.

7 Stephen Hough, *The Bible as Prayer: A Handbook for Lectio Divina*, Mahwah, NJ, Paulist Press, 2007, p. 9.

8 It is not just the South African Archbishops Tutu and Ndungane who speak out against some fellow African, Asian and other conservative spokesmen. For example, Archbishop Peter Akinola, who has spoken out against homosexuality in colourful language and some of whose deeds have threatened schism in the Anglican Communion, is a controversial figure to many other Nigerian clergy and to most pan-African Christian Aids activists.

9 This is my own translation, to avoid the NRSV's clumsy and oddly generic reference to 'humankind'.

Bibliography

Eileen Barker, *New Religious Movements: A Practical Introduction*, London, HMSO Books, 1989.

Enid Blyton, *The Children's Life of Christ*, London, Methuen, 1943 edition.

John Bowker, *Problems of Suffering in Religions of the World*, Cambridge, Cambridge University Press, 1975.

John Bowker, *The Meanings of Death*, Cambridge, Cambridge University Press, 1993.

John Bowker, *The Sense of God*, Oxford, Oneworld, 1995.

Owen Chadwick, *The Victorian Church Part II*, London, Adam and Charles Black, 1972 edition.

Nirad Chaudhuri, *Scholar Extraordinary: The Life of Friedrich Max Müller*, New Delhi, Oscar Publications, 1996 edition.

Kenneth Cracknell, *Our Doctrines: Methodist Theology as Classical Christianity*, Calver, Cliff College Publishing, 1998.

Kenneth Cracknell, ed., *Wilfred Cantwell Smith: A Reader*, Oxford, Oneworld, 2001.

Kenneth Cragg, *The Call of the Minaret*, Oxford, Oneworld, 2000 edition.

Richard Dawkins, *The God Delusion*, London, Bantam Press, 2006.

John Drane, *What Is the New Age Saying to the Church?*, Grand Rapids, Zondervan, 1991.

Farid Esack, *The Qur'an: A User's Guide*, Oxford, Oneworld, 2005.

Martin Forward, *Jesus: A Short Biography*, Oxford, Oneworld, 1998.

Martin Forward, *A Bag of Needments: Geoffrey Parrinder and the Study of Religion*, Bern, Peter Lang, 1998.

Martin Forward, *The Failure of Islamic Modernism?: Syed Ameer Ali's Interpretation of Islam as a Religion*, Bern, Peter Lang, 1999.

Martin Forward, *Religion: A Beginner's Guide*, Oxford, Oneworld, 2001.

Martin Forward, *Inter-religious Dialogue: A Short Introduction*, Oxford, Oneworld, 2002.

Bibliography

John Lewis Gaddis, *The Landscape of History: How Historians Map the Past*, Oxford and New York, Oxford University Press, 2002.

Lenn E. Goodman, ed., *Ibn Tufayl's Hayy Ibn Yaqzan*, Los Angeles, gee tee bee, 1996 edition.

Paulos Mar Gregorios, *A Light Too Bright: The Enlightenment Today*, New York, SUNY, 1992.

Alfred C. Haddon, *History of Anthropology*, London and New York, The Knickerbocker Press, 1910.

Sam Harris, *Letter to a Christian Nation*, New York, Knopf, 2006.

John Hick, *God and the Universe of Faiths: Essays in the Philosophy of Religion*, Oxford, Oneworld, 1994 revised edition.

John Hick, *An Autobiography*, Oxford, Oneworld, 2002.

Christopher Hitchens, *God Is Not Great: How Religion Poisons Everything*, New York and Boston, Twelve, 2007.

Morna D. Hooker, *Paul: A Short Introduction*, Oxford, Oneworld, 2003.

Stephen Hough, *The Bible as Prayer: A Handbook for Lectio Divina*, Mahwah, NJ, Paulist Press, 2007.

Walter Isaacson, *Einstein: His Life and Universe*, New York, Simon & Schuster, 2007.

Philip Jenkins, *The New Christendom*, Oxford, Oxford University Press, 2003.

Philip Jenkins, *The New Faces of Christianity*, Oxford, Oxford University Press, 2006.

Gabriel Josipovici, *The Book of God: A Response to the Bible*, Yale, Yale University Press, 1988.

Ursula King, *Christian Mystics: Their Lives and Legacies Throughout the Ages*, Mahwah, NJ, Hidden Spring, 2001.

Joseph Klausner, *Jesus of Nazareth*, London, George Allen & Unwin, 1928.

Klaus Klostermaier, *Hindu and Christian in Vrindaban*, London, SCM, 1969.

Bernard Manning, *The Hymns of Wesley and Watts*, Salem, Schmul Publishing Co, Inc., 1987 edition.

Alister McGrath, *Christian Spirituality*, Oxford, Blackwell, 1999.

Alister McGrath, *The Twilight of Atheism: The Rise and Fall of Disbelief in the Modern World*, London, Rider & Co., 2005.

Diana McVeagh, *Gerald Finzi: His Life and Music*, Woodbridge, Boydell, 2005.

Daniel B. Merrick and David P. Polk, eds., *Chalice Hymnal*, Chalice Press, St. Louis, 1995.

Charles F. D. Moule, *The Origins of Christology*, Cambridge, Cambridge University Press, 1977.

Seyyid Hossein Nasr, *Islamic Science: An Illustrated Study*, Westerham, World of Islam Publishing Ltd., 1976.

Henri Nouwen, *The Wounded Healer*, New York, Bantam Dell, 1994 edition.

Geoffrey A. Oddie, *Imagined Hinduism: British Protestant Missionary Constructions of Hinduism, 1793–1900*, New Delhi, Thousand Oaks and London, Sage, 2006.

Albert Outler (ed.), *The Works of John Wesley*, vol. 3, Nashville, Abingdon Press, 1986.

Geoffrey Parrinder, *Mysticism in the World's Religions*, Oxford, Oneworld, 1995 edition.

Alan Race, *Christians and Religious Pluralism: Patterns in the Christian Theology of Religions*, London, SCM, 1993 revised edition.

Hanna Rosin, *God's Harvard: A Christian College on a Mission to Save America*, Orlando, Harcourt, 2007.

Richard E. Rubenstein, *When Jesus Became God: The Struggle to Define Christianity During the Last Days of Rome*, San Diego and New York, Harvest, 1999.

E. P. Sanders, *The Historical Figure of Jesus*, Harmondsworth, Penguin, 1996.

Annemarie Schimmel, *Mystical Dimensions of Islam*, Chapel Hill, University of North Carolina Press, 1975.

Albert Schweitzer, *The Quest of the Historical Jesus*, Mineola, Dover Publications, 2005 edition.

Ninian Smart, *The World's Religions*, Cambridge, Cambridge University Press, 1998.

Wilfred Cantwell Smith, *Modern Islam in India*, London, Gollancz, 1946 edition.

Wilfred Cantwell Smith, *Questions of Religious Truth*, New York, Charles Scribner's Sons, 1967.

Wilfred Cantwell Smith, *The Meaning and End of Religion*, London, SCM, 1978 edn.

Victor J. Stenger, *God: The Failed Hypothesis. How Science Shows that God Does Not Exist*, Amherst, Prometheus Books, 2007.

Helmut Thielicke, *The Waiting Father*, London, HarperCollins, 1981.

Geza Vermes, *The Religion of Jesus the Jew*, London, SCM, 1993.

Timothy Ware, *The Orthodox Church*, Harmondsworth, Penguin, 1993.

Frank Whaling, *Christian Theology and World Religions: A Global Approach*, London, Marshall, Morgan & Scott, 1986.

Michael York, *Pagan Theology: Paganism as a World Religion*, New York, New York University Press, 2003.